D1534740

2/6

SPAIN IN REVOLT

SPAIN IN REVOLT

A HISTORY OF THE CIVIL WAR
IN SPAIN IN 1936
AND A STUDY OF ITS SOCIAL
POLITICAL AND ECONOMIC CAUSES

by

HARRY GANNES
and
THEODORE REPARD

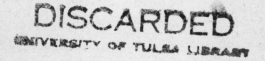
LONDON
VICTOR GOLLANCZ LTD
1936

Printed in Great Britain by
The Camelot Press Ltd., London and Southampton

To those who died
that Spanish democracy might live

" A republic in Spain will give the voice of vigilance to Europe, and vigilance spoken to kings is peace. . . . Danger ? Not any. Spanish citizenship is Spanish strength; democratic Spain is the Spanish citadel.

" If Spain is reborn a monarchy, she will be insignificant.

" If reborn a republic, she will be great."

VICTOR HUGO, 1868.

FOREWORD

THE IMPORTANCE OF SPAIN at the present moment is perhaps equalled only by the lack of accounts, reliable or otherwise, explaining the historical roots of revolt. Especially neglected is the period since the establishment of the Second Republic on April 14, 1931. The existing literature on modern Spain is extremely limited and inadequate, even in Spanish, and especially in English. There is no coherent, systematic account of the history of Spain since 1933 in any language.

We have been guided more by the aim of explaining the immediate background of the fascist revolt of July 17, 1936 than by the aim of doing entire justice to the long and complicated history of Spain. For this reason, the period since 1931 occupies by far the largest portion of the present work. For the last five years we have had the opportunity of following developments in Spain as part of our daily work.

We are especially indebted to Herbert Rosenblum, Minerva Friedman, Pearl Roth, and Dorothy Sapan Draper for research and general assistance.

H. G.
T. R.

CONTENTS

Book I

Book II

BOOK I

CHAPTER I

UPHEAVAL

SPAIN WAS EXPLODED into the rapid and rising stream of European politics by the July 17, 1936 fascist-monarchist uprising against the Republic. Whatever happens now in Spain will have instantaneous repercussions in Europe and by that token upon the entire world. Having escaped participation in the World War, Spain bids fair to offer a pretext for the next. The Iberian Peninsula, so long slumbering as a potent world factor, is now amply making up for lost time. Spain is becoming a pivot on which the world may turn either its fascist or democratic side to the rising sun of the future.

Isolated from Europe not only by the Pyrenees but by the gulf of economic backwardness, Spain is in Europe but not of Europe. Mountain ranges split the country into isolated provinces, not yet adequately bridged by railroads or motor roads. Aragon, Castile, Portugal, Navarra, Catalonia were independent states for centuries. Portugal to-day is a separate nation with a fascist-like dictatorship.

Spain, after France, is the largest European nation in area. Its population of 24,583,096 is unevenly scattered. The variation in density of population per square mile is extreme, the industrial centre around Barcelona numbering 684·2 people per square mile, while Soria has only 39·7. It comprises eleven thirteenths of the Iberian Peninsula, Portugal covering the rest. It contains 190,050 square miles, and with the Balearic and Canary Islands, 196,607 square miles. Thus it is about twice the size of Great Britain and a little larger than the combined areas of the states of New York, New Jersey, Pennsylvania, Ohio, and Indiana.

Travellers, as well as sociologists, see in Spain a land of violent contrasts. Rising mountains of Alpine grandeur contrast with the huge valleys and plains. The lowlands vary from beautifully verdant fields to vast dreary expanses of uniformly parched, desert-like tracts. Among the people the same clashing contrasts are maintained. Fabulously rich landowners, feudal lords over huge domains, live side by side with millions of land-hungry peasants. In the bosom of the Church, too, abrupt dividing lines are revealed: parish priests who are little better than beggars live in the shadows of the great mansions of the fabulously rich princes of the Church. In the army there are highly paid generals, and officers who do not receive enough to pay for food. Culturally the contrasts are equally sharp. Spain has its share of world-famous scholars, scientists, writers, and intellectual leaders, while 45·46 per cent of the population can neither read nor write.

Spain's geographic position in Europe has always been one of the greatest importance. The Iberian Peninsula is situated at the cross-roads of Africa, Europe, and the route to the Near and Far East. Great Britain long ago realised that the position of Gibraltar was the key to the route to India and took the " Rock." Italy and Germany still conspire to obtain Spain's equally strategic African colonies and the Balearic and Canary Islands. Since the conquest of Ethiopia, when war was barely averted between Great Britain and Italy, domination of the Mediterranean has become one of the prime questions of the world's future. Who controls Spain dominates the western entrance—Europe's main gateway to the Mediterranean. The Mediterranean is the British Empire's " life line," Europe's entrance to the Near and Far East, to northern and western Africa, the most vital seaway in the world. Spain's future form of government and social order will be a portent of war or peace.

Fundamental in the problems facing Spain, no matter what the political form of its State, is its unsolved agrarian revolution. Agriculture, involving

Bs

more than half the population, accounting for half of its income, has never been freed from feudal fetters. And without that freedom, growth of any kind, not to say social progress, is impossible. Until the grip of the feudal landlords is broken, the peasantry cannot become free citizens of a democratic Republic. The soil remains, then, as the permanent breeding-ground of reactionary landlordism, the aristocracy, and the hope of monarchical restoration. The terrible subjection of the country population continues. Without a solution of the agrarian question Spain cannot also solve its national question, the striving for national autonomy of the Basque, Galicia, and Catalonia. So long as the land question remains unsettled, it acts as an anchor on the aspirations of the modern proletariat in Spain. Industry, no matter how relatively advanced, still remains subordinated to the backwardness of the countryside. Capitalism, placed over feudalism like a thick plaster of cosmetic on a corpse, is subordinated to the semi-feudal nature of agriculture.

Other countries met this root problem when the rhythm of history's march favoured the rapid development of capitalism on the ruins of the old feudal order. France, classically, solved that problem which Spain now faces by the sweeping revolution of 1789–93. The lords of the manor were overwhelmed, the land distributed among the peasantry of France, and capitalism was permitted to flourish. The United States, in its own special way, first traversed this path by the revolution of 1776, and then by the Civil War of 1861. In England the Cromwellian wars served this purpose. Other nations have solved the problem variously. In the Soviet Union, where it was most recently achieved, the outcome was the creation of a new society—Socialism.

Failing in the solution of the land question in Spain, there can be no ultimate settlement of the burning problems of Church, State, army, democracy, and industrial and cultural progress.

CHAPTER II

HISTORICAL ROOTS OF REVOLUTION

A RAPID GLANCE over the salient features of Spain's reolutionary history will be of immense help in placing the 1936 Civil War in proper perspective.

Until the year 711 the development of Spain was similar to that of other feudal western European countries. In 711 the Moslem invasion overflowed the peninsula. Not until the middle of the fourteenth century was the threat of repeated Moorish invasion finally ended. And not until the middle of the fifteenth century were the last descendants of the Moors driven from Granada.

Moorish domination and culture left a deep imprint on Spain in the flourishing agriculture, the handicrafts, arts, and sciences. The struggle to oust the Africans, with which went the brutal expulsion of the Jews, left Spain further divided, impoverished, and the prey of the feudal lords. Spain from the height of the Moorish days to the worst period of its own monarchy, declined in population from about 30,000,000 to 8,000,000.

Also the protracted wars for the expulsion of the Moors further accentuated the regionalism of a country already distinctly sectionalised.

The close of the period of the great reconquest left Spain divided between two main states: the kingdom called, for short, Castile and León, on the west of the Iberian range and south of the Guadarrama Mountains; and the kindom called, for short, Aragon, on the eastern slope of the Iberian hills and on the great central table-land.

Christianisation occupied Spain from the conclusion of the reconquest of the country down to the union of the crowns of Castile and Aragon by the marriage of Ferdinand and Isabella in 1469. Christianisation was not only a spiritual process of religious indoctrinisation; it was the ideological extirpation of Arab culture and influence to ensure the political domination of the European feudal rulers and to hasten the establishment of an absolute monarchy. While the absolute monarchy was never achieved, the complete domination of the Church was an outstanding and lasting success. The importance of the Church's role lies in the Moslem character of the invasion which had so deeply sunk its superior cultural roots into the soil of Spain. The ruthless extirpation of Moorish and Jewish religious remnants reached its climax in the cruel and horrifying Inquisition.

Ferdinand of Aragon and Isabella of Castile

began the process of Spanish unification. Their reign was also marked by the discovery of America by Columbus, with the financial aid of Isabella. That opened the way for the pillage of the American colonies. Searching exclusively for gold and silver, the parasitic nature of the colonial conquest was obvious. Cortez himself frankly admitted that he was seeking gold and precious metals only and was unconcerned about the cost in native lives or destruction of the Aztec civilisation. The wealth stolen by the *conquistadores* was squandered on feudal luxuries in Spain. With the extensive plunder, a feudal governmental administration was set up.

Lack of national cohesion made the uniform development of the bourgeois revolution difficult and prolonged.

The decline of Spanish agriculture and handicrafts, as well as of the admirable systems of irrigation introduced by the Moors, pushed Spain backward despite the flood of gold from the mines of Montezuma.

Spain's domination by the " illustrious " house of Habsburg after the death of John, the only son of Ferdinand and Isabella, began a sorry period when the country became the chief champion of the Catholic Counter-Reformation. Charles I of this house simultaneously assaulted two pillars of Spanish freedom : first, the old Goth assemblies, and, secondly, the combination of the hereditary and elective municipalities, which had existed almost without interruption from the Roman epoch. In 1521, Charles I finally succeeded in defeating the *comuneros* (municipalities of Villalar). The municipalities in 1931, after nearly four centuries, were able to turn the tide against King Alfonso XIII.

Passage of control of the monarchy from the Habsburgs to the Bourbons in the eighteenth century is not of fundamental importance in the political development of Spain.[1]

While capitalism began to grow elsewhere, industrial capital was extremely slow in developing in Spain. Agriculture, in fact, was abandoned for pasturage. Industry was fettered by the great landlords, and with its backwardness the bourgeoisie was slow in emerging. The stream of wealth from the colonies had increased merchant but not industrial capital, and this accounted for the more rapid circulation of goods without increase in production. One fifth of the population was composed of government officials. There was generally

---

[1] From a medical and psychiatric viewpoint it has been argued, of course, that the change to the Bourbons was distinctly retrogressive. Gonzalo de Réparas, hijo, in his book *Los Borbónes de España, historia patológica de una dinastìa degenerada* (*The Bourbons of Spain, the Pathological History of a Degenerate Dynasty*), classifies the Bourbons as follows: Felipe V, mentally unbalanced and sensual; Fernando VI, mad and impotent; Carlos III, almost normal; Carlos IV, imbecile; Fernando VII, excessively sensual, cruel, and sanguinary; Isabel II, nymphomaniac; Alfonso XII, tubercular.

a stubborn growth of retarding factors, the
Church and the army, while the embryo bourgeoisie, which in other countries stood in the van
of revolution in this period, was very late in
maturing. The treaty of Utrecht, 1813, which
made the country a virtual tributary of England,
revealed the decadence of Spain in all its brutality.

It was not until 1714 that Catalonia, the most
advanced industrial section of the peninsula, was
conquered. Catalonia was the Venice of Spain, a
flourishing merchant republic. It had carried on
trade with the Orient, Africa, and the rest of
Europe. It had early developed factories. This
accounts for the higher degree of capitalist development in Catalonia, as compared with the rest of
Spain to-day; the maturity of the working class;
its separate national development; and its role
as the Ireland of Spain, combining the struggle
against feudalism with the fight for its national
liberation.

During the past several hundred years Spanish
history records a continuous increase in revolutionary outbreaks. There were constant, though
ineffectual, peasant insurrections; repeated efforts
to limit the power of the monarchy, to wipe out
feudal fetters, and to establish a republic. Finally,
with the rebellion of 1854, there appeared more
prominently and thenceforth in a conclusive
position the modern proletariat. And with the

proletariat's entry into the struggles there were initiated mass strikes and protracted rebellions. The democratic revolution was immeasurably speeded up and aspirations for its socialist transformation introduced.

Throughout these struggles the bourgeoisie rarely acted alone. This characteristic was especially significant in the resistance to the fascist Civil War in 1936. In their earlier days, the liberal merchants and industrial capitalists sought to burst the bonds of feudalism and swung along with certain feudal elements such as exploited peasants or parasitic officers. They were finally forced either to rely on the support and action of the proletariat, or to enter into actual collaboration with the working class.

The Napoleonic invasion of Spain in 1808 hurried the fruition of revolt. Napoleon took advantage of a family clash in the court of Madrid and attempted to put his brother Joseph on the throne of Spain. Spain's reply was the War of Independence. The Pyrenees, it turned out, did not prove to be a barrier high enough to keep back the eighteenth-century revolutionary philosophy of France and Germany.

Assuming primitive and ferocious proportions, the resistance was a bitter surprise for Napoleon's army. The Spanish *guerrilleros* (irregulars), a motley army, worthy ancestors of the People's

Front forces of 1936, made of every rock a fortress,
and an ambush of every mountain crag. One
Spanish writer says they converted their wells
into graves and their cities into cemeteries. Like
an earthquake, the invasion shook the country
into realisation of its national existence. In fighting ostensibly for the King, the people soon began
to lose their devotion to the monarchy.

Though the National Party and the *guerrilleros*,
for the most part, were composed of those steeped
in feudal and Catholic tradition and superstition, a small but influential minority looked to
the popular uprising against the Napoleonic
invasion as a means of regenerating Spain. The
minority represented the rising bourgeoisie, consisting of the city merchants and the earliest
industrial capitalists, lawyers, doctors, writers,
students, and even some priests. Though starting
as a revolutionary campaign, the war ultimately
became reactionary when the prerogatives of the
Church and feudal property were threatened in
the struggle for national liberation.

As directorates of the revolution, juntas, or controlling committees, were set up. Far from breaking with the monarchy, they recognised it. The
juntas, declared Karl Marx, who together with
Frederick Engels intimately studied every phase
of the Spanish revolution in their day, were
born under the same lucky star as the French

Committee of Public Safety. The Committee was favoured in its revolutionary tasks by the necessity of repelling foreign invasion. Under the same compulsion the juntas, too, had a splendid opportunity to put through the necessary measures at home against the feudal aristocracy and the privileges of the Church. They failed in this task, as all other juntas of the Spanish bourgeoisie failed, in carrying the democratic revolution to its conclusion. Out of this failure arose the success of the counter-revolution and the costly delay of the democratic revolution. The junta, Marx concluded, not only did nothing: it prevented others from acting.

The passage of a Constitution at Cádiz in 1812 was also a failure. Ferdinand VII was able on May 4, 1814 to proclaim the dissolution of the Cortes and the abrogation of the Constitution. The most active members of the Cortes were condemned to exile, to the galleys, or to African jails.

Repression of the revolts in the American colonies gave rise to a third attempt at revolt of a military character. In 1819 an expeditionary force under General Rafael del Riego revolted at Cádiz. The uprising failed, though it had serious repercussions in Galicia, Valencia, Zaragoza, Barcelona and Pamplona.

In 1820, because of the chaos that followed the indecisive contest between monarchy and republican allies, Tsar Alexander I of Russia proposed

to the Holy Alliance that intervention be undertaken in Spain, and he graciously offered the use
of his army for the purpose. Objections of France
and England quashed the proposal.

Meanwhile Spain's colonies in America were
successfully breaking all ties with the mother
country and establishing their independence. They
achieved their liberation, not without the help of
Great Britain, which saw in the rupture of the
monopolistic trade ties with Madrid a splendid
opportunity for its own commercial fortunes.
When the wealth from the vast South American
empire stopped flowing, it served to emphasise
the industrial impoverishment of Spain and led to
the harsher exploitation of the workers and
peasants by the feudal lords, now deprived of a
valuable source of foreign income.

Despite defeats, the bourgeoisie of Spain grew
stronger and the aristocracy and monarchy grew
weaker as a result of the loss of the American
colonies. The feudal government was, in time,
forced to grant at least a caricature of a constitution with the Royal Statutes of 1834, 1837, and
1845.

By 1854 the bourgeoisie in its clash with the
monarchy found it had to reckon with the maturing and growing working class. Indications of the
development of capitalist factors multiplied. The
French revolution of 1848 unleashed a general

spirit of liberation throughout Europe. The Spanish bourgeoisie, always politically late, could not take advantage of the favourable historical period. Power passed into the hands of the absolutist, feudal Catholic Party.

Working-class insurrections and riots marked the first months of the significant year 1854. On June 28, General Leopoldo O'Donnell led the Madrid regiments in a serious insurrection. He issued an appeal to the people for a republican revolution. Through fear of the working class, the Spanish industrialists, the middle class, and the Republicans generally, allied themselves with the feudalists, thereby renouncing the achievement of their own democratic revolution. The subsequent revolution of 1868 was the work of a coalition of generals, progressives, and republicans, then called Democrats. They carried along with them the toiling population. Again failure dogged all efforts to create a durable government.

From 1854 to 1870 there was a spurt in Spain's industrial progress. While this increased the motive for a clash between feudalism and rising capitalism, it also added the proletariat as an antagonistic class to the liberal bourgeoisie, though both found co-operation imperative against the monarchy. Yet the political situation as a whole remained confused.

A section of the First International, led by the

founders of Scientific Socialism, Karl Marx and Frederick Engels, had already been established in Spain. It had members in all large cities. The anarchist faction, however, dominated the Spanish movement. Mikhail Bakunin, turbulent anarchist leader, who since 1868 had been a bitter opponent of Marx in the International, won the greatest influence among the Spanish workers. Marxists pointed out that anarchist trends within the labour movement are a reflection of middle-class ideology in the ranks of the working class. They are found chiefly in the more backward capitalist countries, and were especially prevalent in Spain, owing to the peculiar development of capitalism and the labour movement. Spain to-day is the last country still to retain a large and influential syndicalist and anarchist movement, though its character is being drastically modified by rapid political developments.

After the republican defeat of 1871 Don Amadeo of Savoy came to the throne. But Spain was beset with many difficulties. It confronted a revolt in Cuba, a Carlist insurrection, and harassing financial disturbances. Don Amadeo soon retired under the menace of a popular uprising, somewhat as King Alfonso XIII " took a walk " in 1930. Amadeo has ever since been called " the King who went out on strike."

When Spain's first Republic was established by

a military coup in 1873, the Bakuninist movement, because of its contempt for politics and its fervent opposition to *all* forms of State power, resisted participation in the Republic. For that they were severely taken to task by Marx's co-worker Frederick Engels.

" When the Republic was proclaimed in February 1873," wrote Engels, " the Spanish adherents of the Alliance [an organisation which had the largest following among the workers] found themselves in a very difficult position.

" Spain is a very backward country industrially, so that there can be no question at all of an immediate emancipation of the working class. Before it could arrive at that point, Spain must still pass through various preliminary steps in its development and remove a whole series of obstacles from its path.

" To reduce the period of these preliminary steps to the shortest possible lapse of time, to force the obstacles aside rapidly—this is what the Republic offered. But it was only possible to take advantage of this opportunity by the active participation of the Spanish working class in political life. That was the feeling of the mass of the workers, who everywhere insisted on participation in events, on utilisation of the opportunity to act, instead of leaving the field free, as had been done up to now, for the activity and the intriguing of the owning class."

With the failure of the workers, under anarchist influence, to take a more active part in the political life of the Republic, in alliance with the liberal bourgeoisie, as advised by both Marx and Engels, complete power passed into the hands of the Republicans; but they were unable to hold it. A military coup ended the life of Spain's first real Republic. The bourgeoisie again showed itself unable to complete its revolution and end feudal domination.

The house of Bourbon, in the person of King Alfonso XII, regained the throne in 1875. That initiated a new era of anti-monarchical strife, which is still being fought out in the bitterest battles of our own day.

The ease and enthusiasm with which some of the official layers of the lower bourgeoisie swung from Republic to monarchy is the subject of a famous story told in Spain. Soon after Alfonso XII was crowned in the restored monarchy, he visited a small town. The alcalde (mayor) and other municipal authorities in the welcoming committee cheered lustily. They cried: " *Eviva !* " until they were blue in the face. One of them outdid all the rest. He shouted, cheered, and gesticulated wildly and frantically. The King, somewhat sceptical of the genuineness of the reception, turned to the loudest and most vociferous demonstrator. " Take care you don't injure yourself, my good man," he cautioned. " Ah, Your Majesty, this is nothing to the way I thunder when I am not ill," replied the enthusiast. " You should have heard me cheer when the Republic was proclaimed. It was then that I burst a blood-vessel."

CHAPTER III

FROM BOURBONS TO REPUBLICS

KING ALFONSO XIII was born under the sign of death. He was a posthumous child, brought into the world six months after the death of his father, King Alfonso XII. The restored Bourbon monarchy of 1875 remained rickety and uncertain. The death of King Alfonso XII, on November 25, 1885, increased that uncertainty until the posthumous heir was born. Until 1902, a regency ruled. This was the period of the rapid rise of imperialism, when the leading capitalist nations of the world scoured the globe for colonies. The newest imperialist nation, the United States, found the last remaining island colonies of the once great Spanish Empire at its doorstep. The big trusts in the United States, whose avaricious desire for colonial conquest was so enthusiastically sponsored by William Randolph Hearst and the yellow Press, chose Spain as their victim for two reasons: Spain was the weakest European power, and Spanish colonies lay directly in the Caribbean and Far Eastern path of Yankee imperialism.

Spain renounced her rights to Cuba and Puerto Rico and ceded the Philippine and Sulu Islands to the United States as payment for losing the Spanish-American War. Other fragments of her island empire in the Pacific were finally sold.

The Spanish army and navy returned home defeated and bitter. Out of the reverses grew a new spirit among a rising group of intellectual leaders, expressive of the revival of opposition to the monarchy, which was blamed for the catastrophe. The " generation of 1898 " was one of the most illustrious and productive in Spain's history, politically and intellectually.[1]

A turning-point was reached. As always in Spain, because of its arrested development, the full significance of the 1898 debacle did not express itself until much later. Spanish capitalism, deprived of the last of its important colonies, decided to attempt to spur forward its industrial development and to rely on exploitation at home. There occurred a return of capital from the former colonies, and a partial revival of industry set in. Foreign investments in Spain increased. With the enlargement of industry, the influence of the revolutionary Spanish working class was extended.

[1] Among the illustrious names of the " generation of 1898 " were: Miguel de Unamuno, elder philosopher of the period, who in August 1936 turned against the Republic because he considered the masses too immature for further reforms; José Ortega y Gasset, Marcelino Menéndez y Pelayo, Pío Baroja, Azorín, Carmen de Burgos, Blasco Ibáñez, La Pardo Bazán.

But the loss of the colonies was a blow that came at a time when other leading countries were building highly integrated trusts, concentrated banking capital, with superior industry. Spain was hopelessly backward, and the flicker of the monarchical candle with borrowed capitalist light could not last long. By this time, also, the Socialist Party of Spain and the syndicalists had become outstanding in the revolutionary movement.

By 1909 the working class had begun to take a leading—even the leading—role in the struggle against the monarchy. In that year a revolutionary strike in Barcelona was transformed into a nation-wide general strike. The immediate pretext for the strike was labour's protest against the Moroccan war. The actual cause was labour's discontent with its economic conditions combined with the rising anti-monarchical sentiment. After three days of street fighting the government suppressed the strike. Martial law was proclaimed throughout the nation. Francisco Ferrer, an anarchist famed for his educational activities, a vigorous opponent of the Church, which he accused of fostering bestial ignorance and superstition, was arrested. After a drumhead court martial he was executed on October 31, 1909.

Strikes, nevertheless, continued to increase. In March 1916 the General Workers' Union and the National Confederation of Labour unitedly demanded that the government reduce the cost of living. A twenty-four-hour general strike was called on December 18, 1916 which forced considerable concessions from the government. Again, on March 27, 1917, the two foremost unions agreed to call on the workers to join in a general strike for an indeterminate period. Their objective this time was to compel the ruling classes to grant fundamental legislative changes guaranteeing a minimum standard of living. The anti-monarchical tendency was becoming widely prevalent. Even monarchists desiring to modernise the monarchy for its own preservation became sharply critical. With the rising tempo of the working-class struggle, coupled with the republican aspiration of the Spanish bourgeoisie, the abuses of the monarchy stood out in stark relief as Spain's backwardness (despite relative progress) was contrasted with the rapid imperialist development of other big powers.

Don Leopoldo Romeo, editor of *Correspondencia de España*, a personal and political friend of King Alfonso and a perfervid monarchist, in an open letter to the monarch, wrote on October 28, 1917 :

" The army lacks everything that characterises a modern army ; the navy is another faction anchored to the ports ; justice is nothing more than groups of favourites assembled in halls by the will of the proctor; the clergy is a corporation governed by those who are anointed with the

favour of some personage capable of making
canons out of curates, and bishops out of canons;
the bureaucracy is a nursery for the abuse of
power; the estimates have become transformed
into a horn of plenty which is drained in whatever
direction it may please the cacique [local boss];
parliament is a meeting-place where time is wasted.
Spain is nothing but the fief of a monarchist
caucus which begins its actions by tolerating bread
light in weight and ends with the deification of the
idiots."

The extreme instability of the throne following
the outbreak of the World War was seen in the fact
that between March 22, 1918 and September
13, 1923 there were twelve different Cabinets. Each
had been unable to cope with the aggravated
problem of the colonial revolution of the Riffs, led
by Abd-el-Krim, and with the rising working-class
struggle, the growing republican agitation, and
the intensified demand for national liberation of
the Catalonian provinces.

Italy had already experienced the rise of a
Fascist dictator. The words *Fascismo* and *Fascisti*
began to ring strangely but more frequently.
Therefore, when the Spanish monarchy, as the
result of serious military reverses, faced collapse, a
dictatorship was set up as a buffer between popular
indignation and King Alfonso's responsibility.
Indignation reached its peak after the tragedy at

Anual, in Spanish Morocco, in July 1921, which in one day cost the lives of over ten thousand soldiers. A commission of twenty-one parliamentary members was appointed to ascertain responsibility.

Finally, in the summer of 1922, the report of the committee, headed by General Picasso, was presented. Promptly the Council of Ministers suppressed it. An inkling of its harassing contents, nevertheless, reached the people. Implicated in the report were not only the governing and military staff, but the King himself. Among the punishments recommended for the culpable was death for the high commanding generals in Morocco and for several of the ministers in Madrid.

A storm of protest burst over the news that the Picasso report was to be shelved. The King dissolved Parliament. New elections left conditions unchanged. The way was open for a dictator to step in. General Primo de Rivera was the man of the hour, qualified by his demagogic criticism of the monarchy. His previous protest against the butchery of soldiers in Morocco stood him in good stead. Primo de Rivera's slogan was: " Fatherland, Monarchy, Religion." With an iron hand he put an end to the movement which threatened to implicate the King himself. The nobility, the large landowners, the Church dignitaries, the monarchist pensioned mayors, the responsible militarists, all

breathed a sigh of relief at the advent of the Primo
de Rivera dictatorship.

Primo de Rivera's first Cabinet was chosen exclusively from the military. The army officers,
through their *Juntas Militares* (Military Committees) had already gained great influence in the
political life of Spain. De Rivera feared their
meddling in politics and sought to deprive them
of their power by the policy of corruption of the
leading figures. By December 1925 the military
Cabinet was succeeded by the so-called Civil
Directorate, composed of three military men and
five civilians.

Even the Socialist Party had been misled. The
Socialist Party leaders, at that time not cognisant
of the danger of fascism, were opposed to a general
strike, by which it was then possible to thwart
Primo de Rivera's military movement. In fact,
later in the reign of de Rivera, Socialist leaders
accepted posts in the government. The Communist Party, small, and divided by factional fights
at that time, was driven into an illegal, underground existence.

It is erroneous to believe that negotiations with
foreign fascist dictators originated with the counter-
revolution of July 1936. As far back as 1923, the
Spanish dictator, Primo de Rivera, consulted with
Mussolini's envoys for the purpose of countering
British and French policy in Gibraltar, Tangier,

and Morocco. The Treaty of Madrid, signed by Primo de Rivera's Foreign Minister, Santiago Alba, established the basis for friendly co-operation between the dictators of Italy and of Spain. Whether Mussolini then envisioned the conquest of Ethiopia or the contest over the Mediterranean cannot be ascertained. To help develop fascist ideas in Spain, Mussolini sent many well-known Italian Fascists to Madrid to lecture about the wonders of *Fascismo*. Outstanding among these was Stefano Molle, whose lectures in Madrid during the year 1926 were sponsored by Primo de Rivera's dictatorship.

This dictatorship had a weakness absent from Mussolini's and later from Hitler's. It lacked a mass organisational base, such as Mussolini supplied by his Black Shirts and Hitler by his Storm Troopers. Furthermore, the Spanish monarchical shock-absorbers were not yet adept in the important fascist art of demagogy. Gil Robles was to remedy that later, however.

Financial difficulties, continuation of corruption, the accentuated backwardness of Spanish economy, lack of confidence, rising republican sentiment, made Spain an easier prey to the rising economic storm. Spain felt the devastating effect of the crisis of 1929 sooner than the United States, for example. The first political casualty was the fall of the dictatorship in January 1929.

Its main base in the army slipping away under the hammer-blows of the economic crisis and the storm of popular discontent, Primo de Rivera realised the close of his reign was near. On January 26, 1930 he appealed to the army (as his chief parliament) to voice its confidence in him. Stony silence greeted his request. On January 28, 1930 the dictatorship under the personal guidance of Primo de Rivera ended in an abrupt manner; but strenuous efforts were made by the crown to continue the dictatorial rule under less imposing figures, such as General Dámaso Berenguer and Admiral Juan Aznar.

King Alfonso did everything possible to save his toppling crown, tried every political combination that could be used to bring about a government that might maintain the monarchy. The republican movement, however, was rapidly sweeping forward. The cost of living mounted. Primo de Rivera's efforts to satisfy the clergy and the military had increased expenditures, raised taxes and made deficits in the budget. The peseta continued to fall.

With Primo de Rivera gone, the fall of the monarchy could not be far behind.

On August 17, 1930 republican leaders met at Hotel de Londres, San Sebastián. Headed by the extreme Right republican leaders, such as Niceto Alcalá-Zamora, later President of the 1931

Republic; Alejandro Lerroux, later associated with the fascist leader José Maria Gil Robles, Miguel Maura, and others, a pact was drawn up compromising whatever differences there were to attain the common object of the establishment of a republic. They counted on nation-wide general strikes and support of the bulk of the army.

Captain Fermín Galán, a heroic republican figure, author of an idealistic book for the regeneration of Spain, *The New Creation*, on December 12, 1930 led what was known as the Jaca Revolt.

The fact that Captain Galán commenced the revolt prematurely shows the mistrust of the republican officers towards the republican civil leaders, who constantly postponed the hour of revolution. Captain Galán and his associates hoped to confront the republican leaders with a *fait accompli* and thus compel them to act further. The revolt was a miserable failure. Together with Captain Angel García Hernández, Captain Galán was court-martialled and sentenced to death. At the trial he was asked: " Did you have accomplices ? " " Yes," was the reply. " Who are they ? " " Yourselves, cowards ! " shouted the condemned captain.

On February 16, 1931 the King decided to entrust José Sánchez Guerra, formerly one of the leaders of the Conservative Party, with the formation of a government. In 1929 Sánchez Guerra had taken part in an abortive putsch against the dictatorship of Primo de Rivera. He had been imprisoned for ten months and then acquitted by a court martial.

But this ruse did not help. The Second Republic, most fateful in the history of Spain, was already knocking at the gates of history.

CHAPTER IV

THE IMMACULATE REPUBLIC

THE 1931 REPUBLIC was inaugurated in a spirit of over-confidence. Public opinion had overwhelmingly demanded the end of the monarchy. Among the most faithful henchmen of the King the belief gained that the monarchy must necessarily take an extended vacation to recuperate its strength or face complete historical collapse.

The April 1931 municipal elections afforded the people an opportunity to express their political views for the first time in eight years. Eligible voters eagerly awaited the 12th of April. Balloting was for 80,472 municipal officials, with 150,000 candidates entered in the contest. The campaign, ostensibly for seats in city and village councils, was in every sense of the word a national election. Everybody understood that the central issue of the " municipal " elections was *the Republic versus the Monarchy*. " Your vote must be an arrow in the heart of the monarchy," was the slogan of the republicans.

Despite the gerrymandered nature of the election,

which gave the countryside representation out
of all proportion to its population , there was
no doubt that the majority of the 5,446,000 voters
rejected the monarchy. In the provincial capitals
and larger cities the republicans received 972
municipal seats and the monarchists only 595. A
country which its rulers thought was faithfully
monarchical had proclaimed itself republican over-
night.

King Alfonso and his councillors—or rather his
councillors alone—realised that the tottering
throne could be bolstered only by armed force.
To employ violence against the people would be
to risk revolution. The monarchy was sure to go,
and an anti-monarchical revolution in the process
threatened to rid Spain forcibly and completely
of its feudal substructure. The war-horses of the
monarchy convinced the King that bloody suppression of the people would, at that time, be
baiting destiny.

At 6.40 p.m. on April 14 King Alfonso held his
last official conference with his ministers. At 7.30
p.m. the republican leaders, apprised that the
King was about to abdicate, assumed government
functions and set up a provisional Cabinet. That
very same morning Alcalá-Zamora and Count
Romanones frantically pleaded with the King to
depart before evening when the workers left the
factories. Otherwise, they persuasively warned

Don Alfonso, " it might be too late." At nine
o'clock in the evening the King was speeding in
his car towards the French border.

Alfonso never really renounced his right to the
crown. His final statement, published April 17,
may be called his permanent option to the throne
in the event of fascists or monarchists being able
thereafter to seize control in Madrid. In his statement Alfonso admitted that the Spanish people
loved him no longer. He acknowledged that the
king *can* do wrong, conceding that he had made
mistakes. Then he advised Spain it would hear
from him again, saying: " I am King of all the
Spaniards and I am a Spaniard. . . . I renounce
no single one of my rights, which, rather than
being mine, are an accumulated guardianship of
which I shall one day have to render strict
account." Not only, it appeared, was the landed
wealth of Spain an accumulated right, but the
prerogative of ruling the country was also so
regarded by the Bourbons.

The Provisional Republican Cabinet, including
Republicans and Socialists, comprised the follow-
ing: Niceto Alcalá-Zamora, President; Alejandro
Lerroux, Foreign Affairs; Fernando de los
Ríos, Justice; Miguel Maura, Interior; Indalecio
Prieto, Finance; Alvarez de Albornoz, Public
Works; Marcelino Domingo, Education; Manuel
Azaña, War; Santiago Casares Quiroga, Navy;

Diego Martínez Barrios, Economy; Francisco Largo Caballero, Labour.

Of this first Cabinet, the majority remained faithful to the Republic to the very days of the July Civil War. Only Alcalá-Zamora, Lerroux, and Maura ultimately drifted or consciously went over to the side of reaction.

The nation went wild with joy. The spirit that gripped the people was like that of Armistice Day in countries that had participated in the war. Streets were filled with dancing throngs. Guitars hummed late into the night. The people sang, shouted, drank, in their rapture over the flight of the King and the establishment of the Republic. The Civil Guard, policemen of the monarchy, decked itself out with violet ribbons, the colour of republicanism in Spain. Violet banners, violet dresses, violet ties, violet flags, violet signs, appeared everywhere in a profusion of democratic enthusiasm. The people riotously celebrating the first breath of freedom in fifty-six years of monarchy and dictatorship did not touch a single hangman, lackey, or agent of the hated monarchy. The only casualty recorded in the establishment of the Republic was a Jesuit father who hurt himself jumping out of a window.

Among those who administered the oath of the Republic was General Emilio Mola, then chief of the secret police. There was nothing else to do for those who wished to be in on the ground floor of the new government so that they could the better undermine it from within.

The most conservative politicians, the rich land-owners, bankers, generals, dukes, counts, bishops, adventurers, knew the Republic was a reality to be reckoned with, and they were not slow in recognising its provisional government.

After ruling three months the provisional govern-ment was replaced, on June 29, 1931, by the newly elected Cortes. Preparatory to the elections the provisional government had taken a new electoral census. The voting age, which was twenty-five under the monarchy, was lowered to twenty-three. Parliamentary representation was fixed at one deputy for every 50,000 of the population. That allowed for a total of 470. The cities and industrial centres were granted equal representation with the villages and the countryside, which had been favoured under the monarchy. In the elections it was not surprising to find that the Socialists and republicans together won a majority of the deputies. The monarchists presented no ticket, but the Right opposition parties together had sixty deputies.

The next great task of the Republic was writing the aims and will of its founders into a Constitution. Constitutions, as the American, Mexican, and Soviet basic laws have proved, are pivotal
Ds

documents that not only grow out of a revolutionary period, but help to determine its future course. The Spanish republicans were conversant with these facts, and they made the greatest efforts to choose their constitutional committee with that end in view. Luis Jiminez Asuá, a brilliant young Socialist, was named to head the committee which drew up the draft ultimately accepted.

As adopted and proclaimed on December 10, 1931 by the Constitutional Cortes, the Constitution of the Second Republic was, in phraseology at least, an advanced document of the democratic revolution. It even borrowed socialist phrases.

Spain by the new Constitution was declared to be "a democratic Republic of workers of all classes." Church and State were separated. War was renounced as an instrument of national policy. States (or provincial) rights were defined and granted somewhat on the order of the American Constitution. The solution of the national problem was broached. Equality before the law was provided. A period of three years was fixed for ending State grant to the Church. Registration and ultimate abolition of the religious orders hostile to the Republic were ordered. Freedom of religious worship was proclaimed for the first time. Civil rights were granted. The right of freedom of speech, Press, and assemblage, as well as trial by a confidential court, was guaranteed.

" All the wealth of the country, whoever be the owner, is subordinate to the interests of national economy," said the Constitution.

Protection of the workers, and a full programme of socialist legislation, were promised. Unemployment, old-age, disability, accident, and death insurance were indicated. Besides there were provisions for the curbing of child labour, fixing maximum hours of labour and minimum wages, as well as maternity legislation.

Marriage was placed under the special safeguard of the State. It was founded in equality of rights for both sexes. Parents were to be obligated to care for their children and to educate them.

The structure of the government was ostensibly republican and democratic. The government consisted of a one-chamber parliament—a Cortes elected for four years by universal, equal, direct, and secret vote of all citizens regardless of sex who had reached the age of twenty-three. The Constitution further provided for the election of a President for a term of six years by the members of the Cortes sitting jointly with an equal number of popularly elected delegates. The government functioned chiefly through a Prime Minister and his associates in the Cabinet. The Cabinet members were vested with large powers.

The Constitution reflected the extremely weak

part played by the peasantry in the establishment of the Republic. It was devoid of those sweeping agrarian and Church reforms provided by the Mexican Constitution of 1917. Yet the agrarian conditions and Church domination in Mexico were not much different from those of Spain, which had transplanted the Church and latifundia to its Mexican colony. Because of the powerful opposition of the landed interests, an agrarian reform law was not passed until September 1932; but the agrarian revolution was never carried out.

Catalonia, which had proclaimed the independent Catalan Republic, headed by Colonel Francisco Macía, on April 19, finally came to an agreement providing for a semi-autonomous state, to be ruled by the Generalidad at Barcelona.

Niceto Alcalá-Zamora, who had been President of the provisional government, was elected the first President of the regularly constituted government. Alcalá-Zamora was a monarchist until 1923, when he became a republican under the Primo de Rivera dictatorship. This short, white-haired Andalusian lawyer, fifty-four years of age, was a fairly wealthy landowner with an estate near his native village of Priego de Córdoba. Throughout his presidency he resisted the distribution of the estates of the Spanish grandees and landed gentry, the abolition of the religious orders, and the trial of the monarchists and the supporters of the Primo de Rivera regime for their crimes against the people. Early in 1931 the Vatican announced that it was not alarmed over events in Spain as long as Alcalá-Zamora remained President. He obtained a regal entourage for himself. His salary was a comfortable two million pesetas a year.

The Communist Party of Spain took an irreconcilable position towards the Republic. Though it commanded strong proletarian influence in the anti-monarchical movement, before and immediately after the establishment of the 1931 Republic, it resisted the Socialist-Republican coalition and put forward the aim of a workers' and peasants' republic as the only means of solving the democratic revolution. The Communist Party of Spain, formed in 1921, experienced a period of the strictest illegality under the dictatorship of Primo de Rivera, from 1923 to 1931. It likewise suffered frequently from inner party struggles, the most serious of which was the defection of a Trotskyist faction led by Andrés Nin. The Communist Party soon rectified its mistaken negative approach to the Republic. In the June 1931 elections it was able, however, to put up candidates in only 11 of the 70 constituencies; and while in these elections it received only 60,000 votes, by 1933 its vote had gone up to 400,000, and its membership

had jumped from 1,000 just before the establishment of the Republic to 30,000 soon after.

Somewhat as in France following the inauguration of the Blum government after the May
1936 elections, the establishment of the Republic
in Spain was the signal for a widespread round
of strikes. The workers, feeling the breakdown
of the restraint enforced by the monarchy, and
inspired by their new-found freedom, began to
strengthen their trade-union organisations and
forced increases in wages from employers.

CHAPTER V

THE FASCIST THREAT

When the Republic was proclaimed, the vested interests found themselves in a sad state of disorganisation and disrepute. The monarchy had become so rotten that it almost fell of its own weight, without violence. La Voz boasted at the time: "The new regime came into the world immaculate, without a drop of blood." The army was shaken. Primo de Rivera and Berenguer, both top-notch generals, had demonstrated their inability to hold off the inevitable. The Church, the landowners, and the big capitalists found themselves at a loss.

But the newly born Republic followed up its initial advantage very badly or not at all. The republican government in power was more afraid of really crushing reaction than was the reaction of the Republic. Some of the more notorious enemies of the regime were forced into exile, but the old order remained, gasping for second wind.

Freedom of speech under the new Constitution

meant freedom for the monarchists and the grandees and the high churchmen to befoul the Republic with all kinds of abuse. The old powers
were given more freedom of expression and
assembly than the Communists and anarchists.
There were monarchist, clerical, and grandee
representatives in the Cortes itself.

After all, the government mainly changed at the
top. In the villages life went on pretty much as
before. The army was cut in numbers, but the
officers' caste remained. The day of reckoning was
timidly postponed on every important issue.

The reforms of the new regime served to enrage
the reactionaries without disarming them. Whatever changes were made were changes in degree
and not in kind. The cut in the armed forces was
typical. The officers who were forced into retire-
ment (on full pay!) vowed vengeance, while
those who remained constituted the same old
junta. The republicans needed only to make one
misstep, and time would come marching back.

Out of the welter of confusion and conflict
emerged spokesmen of the Right whose counsel
to the embattled reactionaries was that of Adolf
Hitler in Germany and Benito Mussolini in Italy.
They saw that the crash of the monarchy had
consigned to oblivion all those interests, economic
and social, which had been interlinked and de-
pendent upon the monarchy. The Cortes was

cowardly, but the people were aroused and their pressure could not be indefinitely withstood. The labour movement was beginning to prosper and to demand a place in the sun. In 1931 there were 710 strikes: in 1932 there were 830: and in 1933, 1,499.

Fascism loomed as the only means by which the old order could be revived and kept intact. But fascism in Spain had its special features. The backwardness of big industry and the predominance of the Church and the army forced a close union between the fascists, the landowners, the Church, and the officers' junta. The big capitalists and the foreign concessionaires were important but not primary.

The fascism which arose under the Republic was more serious than even the Primo de Rivera variety, which was bad enough. Primo de Rivera depended entirely upon the army while necessity forced him to maintain the monarchy intact. The fascism of the present is based upon identical social interests, but it is unencumbered by the dead weight of the monarchy. Secondly, Primo de Rivera never had to deal with a really powerful, united, and militant labour movement. As a matter of fact, he succeeded in gaining the passive neutrality of the Socialist leaders. On March 28, 1929 Andrés Saborit, the Socialist secretary, declared: " The Socialist Party does not support the present administration. It is only co-operating with the administration to obtain that which is its due." But the fascism of the present faced an altogether different prospect. Especially after 1933, the split in the labour movement began to heal and an unsuccessful coup by the fascists would certainly put their whole social structure in jeopardy.

A few fascist movements arose very early after the beginning of the Republic, slavishly copying the Nazi model. One of these, the Falange Española (Spanish Phalanx), gave a fairly poor imitation of the Hitlerist Storm Troops. Its leader is José Antonio Primo de Rivera, son of the late dictator. De Rivera is known to have conferred with Hitler in the early part of 1934. The Falange merged with another fascist formation, the Juntas de Ofensiva Nacional-Sindicalistas (J.O.N.S.), early in its career.

Primo de Rivera's following was never very large and consisted almost wholly of " *Pistoleros*," or plain gangsters and gunmen, sprinkled with " gentlemen's sons." The J.O.N.S. consisted mainly of déclassé students and white-collar workers. It was the Falange which specialised in breaking up workers' meetings, smashing strikes, and murdering political opponents.

Another fascist organisation of the same type is the Renovación Española (Spanish Regeneration) led by the former monarchist Antonio Goicoechea. Under the dictatorship of Primo de Rivera, Goicoechea had been a leader of the Conservative Right, the most reactionary of all the monarchical parties. Renovación Española never developed into much of a mass movement, and specialised in thuggery.

Funds for the fascists came from Germany and from donations by native millionaires. No secret was made of the fact that Juan March, Spain's richest man and the Republic's No. 1 enemy, was contributing to Primo de Rivera's Falange.

March has had a colourful career as Spain's leading capitalist. He began life as a fisherman on the island of Majorca, and it is claimed that he was illiterate until the age of twenty-one. He made his fortune, estimated at £20,000,000, as a war profiteer by cornering the Spanish tobacco market. At his trial in 1931 it was charged that he bribed the High Commissioner of Morocco and the commander of the Spanish Foreign Legion for the purpose of smuggling tobacco out of Morocco without paying taxes and duty. Alfonso XIII finally decided to give him the tobacco monopoly in order to be able to collect the duty without difficulty.

March paid his way, it is said, with thousand-peseta notes, during the Primo de Rivera dictatorship, and had the effrontery to stand for office in the first election under the Republic. He was elected, but then his troubles as a deputy in a republican parliament began. The Cortes refused to seat him and turned him over to an investigating committee, which, after investigation, committed him to prison on charges of corruption, bribery, and a shooting.

March remained in prison for seventeen months, when he finally escaped because a bribed prison guard was " sorry for him." This was in November 1933. Three months later he came back from Paris, the place of his exile, when the Lerroux government issued an amnesty to all enemies of the Republic.

An anonymous writer in the London *Spectator* reviewed March's career as follows: " It is certain in any case that those who stood in his way, either in private or public affairs, developed a remarkable tendency to tire of life or to seek fresh starts in foreign fields, such as the Americas."

The real development of fascism in Spain had to come from sources closer to the more powerful and respectable vested interests. Its leader was found in the person of José Maria Gil Robles, a young man forty years old, with just the right qualifications, unencumbered with too many scruples.

Gil Robles was raised in the shadow of the " famous generation." Born November 27, 1898, at Salamanca, the son of a pious university professor, he received an excellent education with the Salesians of Don Bosco and took a doctorate in law at the University of La Laguna, where he became Professor of Political Law for a very short time.

In 1923 Gil Robles forsook teaching for the broader field of politics and became associated with the chief clerical and junker organ in Spain, *El Debate*. Gil Robles was made assistant editor of the paper and, more important, the protégé of its powerful director, Angel Herrara Orio. Herrara Orio is reputed to be the brains of the Jesuit order. In the first election under the Republic, Gil Robles was elected one of the twenty-four deputies of the Agrarian Party.

Gil Robles's star began to rise very fast. Through training and inclination, he was an ideal spokesman and defender of the Church. Through a fortunate marriage with one of the daughters of the Count de Revillaggido, one of the three greatest landowners in the country, he was united with the grandees. He was an ideal man to give fascism a Spanish habitat.

His programme was anti-republican from end to end. He opposed separation of Church and State, the rupture with the Vatican, the confiscation of the property of the Church orders, lay education, divorce, land reform, and autonomy

for Catalonia. *El Debate* was his personal organ.
Later, through José Calvo Sotelo, he obtained
a link with the monarchists. When he became
Minister of War in 1935, he brought General
Francisco Franco in as chief of staff and so made
connections with the Spanish Military Union,
which had taken the place of the old officers'
junta.

In the spring of 1932 Gil Robles began to gather
his forces together. Until then he was known as
one of the oustanding young leaders of the Agrarian
Party, the party of the big landowners, clergy
and monarchists. The Agrarians were too cumber-
some for a frontal attack against the Republic,
he thought. He set about organising his own
party, but, while maintaining connections with
the Agrarians, decided to act much more swiftly
and with greater doses of demagogy.

In the spring of 1932, backed by the all-important Herrara Orio, Gil Robles organised the
Acción Católica (Catholic Action), allegedly on
a non-political basis, to defend the interests of
the Church. The idea behind this movement
was to unite all Catholics against the Republican-
Socialist government, irrespective of party lines.
At the same time Herrara's National Action
was transformed into Popular Action, a political
organisation pledged to the same ends as the
Catholic Action.

In February 1933 Gil Robles went a step further and organised the Confederación Española de Derechas Autónomas (Spanish Confederation of Autonomous Right Parties), commonly known by its initials as C.E.D.A. In this organisation he hoped to group together all the landlords threatened by a genuine reform law. The C.E.D.A. soon became his chief weapon against the Republic.

It is significant that Primo de Rivera and Goicoechea, both undisguised fascists, should stem from the monarchy. It is equally significant that Gil Robles should have such close ties with the Church and the landlords. Spanish fascism had to root itself in the social forces which had most to lose by real republican reforms.

CHAPTER VI

THE REPUBLIC IN ENEMY HANDS

THE HONEYMOON PERIOD of the Republic lasted two and a half years, though not without its bitter quarrels. As early as the winter of 1931 the monarchists and other reactionaries knew the worst. And they did not shudder at the prospects. The government, it is true, consisted at that time exclusively of Left democratic parties: Socialist, Radical Socialist, Republican Action, Catalonian Left, and Galician Republican. The other parties had virtually withdrawn. Outside of the government they gravitated closer to the extreme Rightist groups.

Half-hearted as were the attempts of the Republican-Socialist Cabinet to carry out the original programme of the 1931 Republic, certain positive achievements were made. Besides adopting the Constitution, Catalonia was granted a substantial measure of autonomy; formally, Church and State were sundered; Church schools were ordered eliminated; the establishment of a national system of secular public school education was begun;

radical land reforms were outlined; and a vast scheme of social legislation was initiated.

Least was accomplished, however, on the basic agrarian question. Up to the end of 1933, only 80,800 acres of the big estates had been taken over benefiting the ridiculously small number of 5,000 peasants. There were still two and a half million unsatisfied landless farm labourers and half a million of the poorest peasants.

By far the most popular man in the government was Premier Manuel Azaña. No small share of his popularity rested on the fact that he earnestly worked to dislodge the monarchists' hold on the army. His aim, he said, was to save the army as defender of the Republic. But, at least in 1936, Azaña's early measures, as well as his weak efforts after the February elections, proved that historically the army remained true to its original purpose. The Spanish army was always groomed for the protection of the royal house, and to the throne alone did it owe allegiance before the establishment of the Republic.

The year 1933 saw the cleavage between the classes becoming sharper under the Republic. The wage-workers expressed discontent with the gains from the Republic, not only in the matter of democratic liberties, but in the failure to win sufficiently improved living-standards and working-conditions. The strike wave, which had steadily

Es

been growing since the founding of the Republic, by 1933 had involved more than two million workers in six thousand separate walk-outs.

Many of these strikes also were of a political nature. The anarchists on January 8 and 9 and December 8 of 1933 led serious armed putsches. In some districts these armed clashes were mass movements of a revolutionary character. The workers struggled because they believed the Republic was not doing enough; reactionary army officers plotted coups because they believed the Republic was doing too much. The toiling masses sought to hasten the work of the Republic, while the fascists organised to push Spain backwards. What was surprising was, not the fact that militarist attempts at counter-revolution occurred, but that the officers believed they had a chance of succeeding so early in the life of the Republic.

Most serious was the Sanjurjo uprising. The 1936 Civil War was the legitimate heir of the Sanjurjo coup of August 10, 1932. In fact, the same General José Sanjurjo was slated to be Commander-in-Chief in the 1936 fascist uprising. Death in an aeroplane crash on July 18, 1936 removed the most experienced military organiser of the Spanish fascists.

On August 10, 1932 General Sanjurjo seized control of Seville by a *coup d'État*. He then issued a pronunciamento proclaiming himself governor of the province of Andalusia. Provincial officials were removed. General Sanjurjo had not counted on the stubborn resistance of the Seville workers, who blocked his progress though the Madrid government was slow in acting. Sanjurjo escaped, but was arrested in Huelva on August 11. Although tried for treason and sentenced to death, President Alcalá-Zamora reprieved him. After serving a short prison term General Sanjurjo finally went to Germany, where he consulted the Nazis about the proposed plans for the Spanish Civil War.

Critics of the Republic's pusillanimous attitude towards royalists pointed out at the time that many reactionary fascist-minded militarists were safely in hiding in official army posts. For example, it had sufficed for General Sanjurjo to make a verbal declaration of fidelity to the Republic to be appointed Commissioner of Morocco and later Commissioner of Andalusia, where he began his first coup in 1932. From the beginning Sanjurjo ruthlessly persecuted Communists and Socialists in Andalusia and conspired against the Republic.

While Sanjurjo relied on the military weapon to facilitate fascism, the more shrewd Rightist leaders went about the matter in a more solid, if subtle, crafty, and cunning political fashion. The period from the organisation of the C.E.D.A. to February 1936 constitutes a unified epoch in Spanish history. It is the period of the development of a powerful fascist movement, which felt itself grow strong enough to contest for dictatorial power. When the C.E.D.A. was organised, Gil Robles opposed the regime in power. In November 1933, when the Lerroux government came into office, Gil Robles swung over to the support of the government.

Alejandro Lerroux was the acknowledged leader of the Right opposition to the Azaña government. When Gil Robles organised the C.E.D.A. Lerroux was an old hand at opposition politics. He had been the most prominent republican leader under the monarchy, although then a man already well on in years. When the Republic was declared, the sixty-seven-year-old Lerroux, though he despised the monarchy, entered the Republic with the aim of preventing any drastic economic and social changes. A formal end of the monarchy was enough for him.

Lerroux became the first Minister of Foreign Affairs in the provisional government which lasted from April 1931 until the June 28 elections of the same year. Ousted from his post by the Left sweep, Lerroux went back to opposition politics. No monarchist, neither was he a fascist at the time. But his opposition to the left Republican-Socialist coalition put him in line for unity with the extreme Right, headed by the C.E.D.A. and its *Führer*, Gil Robles.

Gil Robles and Lerroux at first worked together on a strictly oppositional basis. Their joint strategy was to delay and sabotage the work of the Cortes to the utmost. Gil Robles's aim was to embarrass and ultimately to overthrow the Republic; Lerroux's game was to keep the Republic safely conservative, to protect the landlords and the prerogatives of the Church. Together they acted, by intricate parliamentary manœuvres, to prevent bills from coming up on the floor of the Cortes. Once on the floor, progressive measures would be endlessly delayed. In some cases parliamentary sabotage was enough to kill bills or delay them for months. Bills passed were hindered in their execution. All of this was predicated upon the hope and expectation—well founded, as it turned out—that the next national election, scheduled for the end of 1933, would throw power to the Rightists.

Through the dilatory tactics of the Lerroux-Robles coalition the Church led a charmed life in the early days of the Republic. Generously the Republic continued to subsidise one of its worst enemies. In 1931 the Republic paid 65,000,000 pesetas to the Catholic Church; in 1932, 42,000,000; in 1933, 24,000,000. And the subsidies continued in one form or another, thanks to the Rightist victory in the November 1933 elections, right on to the February 1936 People's Front sweep.

The law adopted for the protection of the Republic from its royalist and fascist enemies was used more and more against its best friends, the workers.

Disillusionment with the promises of the Republic had become widespread. It was due to the timidity of the Republican-Socialist coalition on the one hand, and to the cunning filibustering, resistance, and parliamentary sabotage of the Lerroux-Robles Right opposition on the other. Gil Robles and his C.E.D.A. lost no time in utilising this discontent by employing the most appealing demagogy. The Rightists began to sense that they could take over the receivership of the Republic.

By June 8, 1933 the breach between the Left and Right republicans over the key Church and agrarian questions had seriously widened. Lerroux had already accused the Azaña Cabinet of favouring the proletariat and the peasantry. On September 13, 1933 Azaña finally resigned the premiership. The Republican-Socialist coalition Cabinet came to an end, and with its demise began the fascist push for power.

The November 19 and December 3, 1933 elections were a windfall for Gil Robles. Though they did not give the Right an overwhelming victory, they delivered a crippling blow to the Republican-Socialist coalition. Socialist seats in the Cortes were reduced from 114 to 58. The Radical Socialists, who had 55 before, were completely wiped out, and Azaña's Left Republicans dropped from 30 to 5. The strongest single party was that headed by Lerroux, the Radicals, which received 105 seats in the new Parliament. Gil Robles's Popular Action Party won 62 seats; the Agrarians, 88; and the Monarchists, 43.

As the previous spokesman for the Right-Centre opposition, Lerroux was the logical leader of the incoming government. Gil Robles categorically refused to enter the Cabinet, though its life was in his hands. Instead he gave Lerroux conditional support.

Both the results of the November elections and the choice of Lerroux as Prime Minister pleased the Vatican. *El Debate*, Gil Robles's own organ, had already declared: " The great victory of our candidates exceeds even our expectation," and it was able to add, echoing *L'Osservatore Romano*, mouthpiece of the Vatican, that the Church now had the " opportunity to live in the Spanish Republic with dignity, respected in its rights and the exercise of its divine mission."

The new Lerroux government, under pressure of Gil Robles, took steps to negate the actions of the early days of the Republic. Government declarations made it obvious that Lerroux intended to revise the whole of the achievements in social legislation. Lerroux proposed continuance of State aid to the rural clergy. He promised not to close any more religious schools, and to revise the agrarian laws of 1932. At the same time amnesty for exiled royalists was rushed through the Cortes. Among the returning monarchists were Juan March, José Calvo Sotelo, the most ardent and outspoken of all, and Count de Guadelhorce, a powerful and influential landowner. The return of the exiles enabled Gil Robles to cement a powerful alliance with royalist politicians, particularly Calvo Sotelo, who had served as Minister of Finance under the Primo de Rivera dictatorship. When the Republic was proclaimed, he fled to Paris. Although elected a deputy to the Cortes from the monarchist constituency of Orense, in Galicia, in the 1933 elections, he did not take his seat until 1934 after the amnesty law was signed. Then there began a partnership with Gil Robles which matured and lasted until the July Civil War. In fact, Sotelo's assassination, on July 13, 1936, precipitated the fascist revolt prematurely.

Lerroux, under the prompting of Gil Robles, continued to govern by the method of decrees and the operation of the Law of the Defence of the Republic, an anti-monarchical measure, against the republican and revolutionary proletarian parties.

Besides its retrogressive social measures, the

Lerroux government devoted itself to curbing the autonomy of Catalonia. The Right-Centre coalition, however, had over-estimated its strength. Catalonia began to rally its forces for the January 14, 1934 Generalidad elections to rebuff Madrid's efforts to abolish its national independence. Manuel Azaña played a particularly active part in the Catalonian election campaign. The result was an overwhelming victory for the Esquerra (the Catalan Left Nationalist Party), headed by Luis Companys. Catalonia served notice on Lerroux and Gil Robles that it would brook no infringement of its autonomous rights.

Meanwhile trouble was brewing in the Lerroux-Robles parliamentary coalition. The Centre and Right could not agree on how far the retrogressive steps should go within the Republic.

Because the President of the Republic would not sign an omnibus amnesty bill pardoning nine thousand royalists and other reactionary opponents of the Republic, and because of the strong opposition to the cynical restoration of all lands to the grandees, the Lerroux Cabinet resigned on April 25, 1934. Thereupon the Cabinet headed by Ricardo Samper was formed on April 28, with a Centre-Right complexion. While Gil Robles did not withdraw his support from the Samper Cabinet, he put his greatest emphasis on organising mass fascist groups outside of Parliament. In fact, throughout this period Gil Robles strove hard to gain a real mass base for the C.E.D.A. coalition. Demagogy and the huge Church funds were his main instruments. He actually began increasingly to speak about the necessity of dividing the land and breaking up some of the biggest estates, though in Parliament he sponsored measures to protect the big landowners. He made desperate efforts to organise the Catholic peasantry and Catholic trade unions. But while his extreme demagogy earned him the suspicion of the Agrarians, it did not win him the mass base he desired.

On April 22, Gil Robles decided to make a public exhibition of his mass strength. For four months his organisations, the C.E.D.A., the Catholic Union, the Juventud Acción Popular (the youth section of the Popular Action Party), exerted all their efforts to organise a mass demonstration at the Escorial Palace near Madrid. Gil Robles's lieutenants had promised that at least 50,000 positively would be present. A counter-demonstration, and a twenty-four-hour general strike in Madrid dampened the ardour of Gil Robles's followers. Impartial observers estimated that only between 15,000 and 20,000 were present, not an impressive mass force compared to the huge trade-union, Socialist, Communist, Left Republican, and anti-fascist demonstrations for which Madrid was famous. The fascist slogans at

the Escorial were typical : " War on Class War " ;
" Work for All " ; " Down with Parliamentarism" ;
" Down with Dictatorship " ; " Up with the People
Organically Incorporated into a State."

While the Madrid government was travelling
further to the right, Catalonia was rapidly moving
to the left. Among the acts passed by the Catalan
Generalidad during this period, one which was
to prove the pretext for the fall of the Samper
government, and the provocation for the October
1934 workers' armed uprising, dealt with the
agrarian question. The Generalidad legislated to the
effect that there must be a division of the land into
small tracts of a size no larger than the farmer and
his family could till. The occupants of the farm,
it was further provided, must themselves do two
thirds of the labour required. For the remaining
third they could hire wage-labourers. All previous
feudal contracts, whereby the peasants paid
seignorial fees, were abolished. The minimum lease
had to be for a six-year period, with provisions
for its extension. After eighteen years of work the
peasant had the right to purchase the land under
lease.

Agrarian unrest had already gripped the country
as a whole. The Socialist Federation of the Soil
called a strike of two million agricultural labourers
to begin at the time of the June harvest. They
appealed to the syndicalist agricultural workers'

union to join with them. Division among the workers, plus more energetic action on the part of the government in suppressing unrest in the countryside than it ever showed in enforcing the agrarian laws, rendered the strike a failure, though it only intensified agrarian discontent.

From the outset the Samper Cabinet did not satisfy the Rightists. Gil Robles saw popular sentiment swinging left-ward, and he decided something drastic had to be done to move faster towards fascism. Samper proved to be a less pliable tool than Lerroux.

On October 1, 1934 the death warrant of the Samper Cabinet was pronounced by Gil Robles in a speech bitterly critical of Samper's programmatic address to the Cortes. " Weak and humiliating " is the way the Jesuit politician branded Samper's declaration. Gil Robles destroyed the Samper Cabinet with the full realisation that it would lead to civil war. As if by prearrangement, two members of the Cabinet, José Maria Cid, Minister of Communications, and Filberto Villa Lobos, dramatically walked out. The crash of the Samper government was the signal for a quick-step to fascism.

The proletariat of Spain accepted the challenge on the streets.

CHAPTER VII

UPRISING IN OCTOBER

OCTOBER 1934 will always live in the memory of Spain as the period of the workers' heroic answer to the initial attempt to inaugurate a fascist dictatorship. Deliberately, on October 1 the fascist cliques, headed by the C.E.D.A., aimed at provoking civil war by putting their men in the new Lerroux Cabinet. Faced with a point-blank threat of a fascist dictatorship on the Italian and German model, the Spanish workers decided to wage a desperate battle. Once in the fight, they sought to take the initiative. They tried to counter the danger of a fascist dictatorship by the establishment of a workers' and peasants' republic.

Long after the event Gil Robles, in reply to accusations that he had purposefully provoked the October uprising, retorted; " True, I knew that if the representatives of my party joined the government, it would lead to civil war. But let us not be naïve. To wait two or three months would have meant suicide. Spain would have become one vast Asturias and we should have had soviets in Spain to-day."

What was the relation of forces in Spain just
prior to the October uprising ? Having won two
thirds of the seats in the 1933 parliamentary
elections, the Right-Centre bloc, steered by Gil
Robles, was able to consolidate its strength. While
the Right and the Centre were achieving unity for
fascist aims, the workers' movement was advancing
much more slowly to a united outlook and action.

The working class was in a transitional stage,
soon to be marked by two periods of crisis, each
to be followed by extremely speedy development
along the stony path towards proletarian unity.
On the eve of October the majority of the Spanish
industrial proletariat outside of Catalonia was
under the influence of the Spanish Socialist Party,
more particularly the Left wing of that party, led
by the ever more popular Largo Caballero. In
Catalonia, however, consistent with the erratic
development of the Spanish labour movement
and the deep early roots of anarchism, the anarcho-
syndicalist National Confederation of Labour
(C.N.T.) and the Federación Anarquista Ibérica
(Iberian Anarchist Federation) remained dominant among the working class, resisting unity and
advocating unconcern as between the existing
Republic and the danger of a fascist dictatorship.

The Communist Party persistently continued to
raise its chief slogan of the realisation of a united
front against fascism. The success of those tactics

in France had particularly spurred the Spanish Communist Party. Negotiations with the Socialists at first proved fruitless, because the Socialist Party was already supporting a united-front form of organisation, known as the Workers' Alliance. Therefore the Socialist Party rejected the Communist proposal for the formation of a formal united front between the two parties and urged the Communist Party to enter the Workers' Alliance. After severe criticism of the Workers' Alliance for its failure to devote more political and organisational attention to the majority of Spain's toilers— that is, the peasantry—the Communist Party joined the Alliance in September 1934.

While the Communists agreed to support the ultimate aim of " All Power to the Alliances," they at the same time strongly urged the adoption of a minimum immediate programme to rally the broadest masses for an economic war against the strongholds of fascism, which alone could ensure political victory. That immediate programme provided for the following : (1) the confiscation of the land belonging to the big landowners and the Church, and its distribution among the peasants, without compensation to the wealthy landlords; (2) the disarming of all fascists; (3) government control over industry and the banks; (4) the forty-hour week, while maintaining the wages paid for the forty-eight-hour week; (5) the introduction of social and unemployment insurance; (6) punishment of large-scale speculators and usurers, and the confiscation of their property for the benefit of the unemployed; (7) the annulment of all debts owed by the peasants and small shopkeepers to the banks; (8) the liberation of the oppressed nationalities of Catalonia, Biscay, and Galicia, and the recognition of the independence of Morocco.

Frankly dreading the spectre of working-class unity, the Rightists decided that civil war must come before the centripetal force of proletarian unity attracted the peasant allies into an unbeatable anti-fascist bulwark.

Still engrossed in perfecting their proletarian unity, the Spanish workers had not yet sufficiently reached out to the broad People's Front idea of Republican-Socialist-Communist-Anarchist anti-fascist unity.

Fully realising that Gil Robles's action of October 1 signified the fascists were bent on establishing the first phase of the Spanish fascist dictatorship, and that civil war was the only way to avert or at least cripple this move, the Workers' Alliance on October 4 and 5 issued a call for a general strike throughout Spain.

Communist, Socialist, and many non-party workers responded to the appeal. The anarcho-syndicalists were racked by uncertainty, indecision, and even hostility to the strike call. To have

remained inert at this time would have encouraged
the newly formed Lerroux-Robles government to
adopt more stringent fascist measures, depending
on the temper of the anti-fascist resistance and the
risk of revolution run in the process of erecting a
dictatorship.

The industrial centres of the country were immediately paralysed by the general walk-out. In many
places the general strike became an armed insurrection against fascism. Actual fighting, however, was heaviest in Asturias, Biscay, León,
Madrid, and Catalonia.

The October anti-fascist uprising was hampered
at the very beginning, however, by the lack of
solid unity of the working class and by the sporadic
nature of the outbreak. Nevertheless, as the outcome showed, it prevented the introduction of
fascism, inspired the workers and peasants to the
most heroic deeds, and finally led to a turning of
the tide for the anti-fascist People's Front in the
February 1936 elections. Labour unity, weak at
the beginning of the fight, came out of the fire of
battle like forged steel, which required only
tempering and pointing.

No centralised plan had been evolved to guide
the scattered October insurrectionists. In scores of
cities and villages, nevertheless, the workers in
their battles against the fascists seized control of
local power.

Fs

October can be described more accurately as a series of provincial insurrections. Intimately connected was the simultaneous move in Catalonia for national independence. October was not a concerted nation-wide uprising for proletarian power. Largo Caballero later declared that the aim of October was to frighten the bourgeoisie away from fascism, and not to establish proletarian rule in Spain. The embryo soviets that were set up were restricted to Asturias, which was politically and organisationally more mature than the rest of Spain, even than advanced Madrid.

The October events are often inaccurately referred to as the Asturian Revolt because of the spectacular fifteen-day siege of the Asturian miners. The Asturian people, as far back as the days of the Roman conquest and the Moorish invasion, were noted for their bravery. Both the October fighting and the Civil War of 1936 showed to the world that the heroism of the Asturian people, dating from antiquity, lives among the revolutionary miners of to-day. With breathless amazement newspaper readers everywhere followed the death-defying exploits of the dynamite-armed miners in the fight against the fascists in Gijón, Oviedo, Irun, and San Sebastián during the 1936 Civil War. For these miners, that fighting was an inevitable continuation of the October 1934 Civil War.

Oviedo, the scene of savage warfare in the 1936 fighting, together with a large portion of Asturias, was in the hands of the insurgent workers for fifteen days during October 1934. Notwithstanding the fact that there was no respite in the battle during any minute of that period, a rudimentary form of a Workers' and Peasants' Provincial Government was set up.

Law and order were maintained. Strenuous efforts were made to continue industrial production, to keep stores open, to provide for the distribution of food and the other necessities of life. A Workers' Militia was recruited. Decrees were issued in the name of the Asturian Workers' and Peasants' Government, or under the signature of the local Revolutionary Committees. Munitions factories were occupied, and with indefatigable courage the besieged workers set to work to manufacture the necessary ammunition to conduct the war against the superior government forces.

The heroism of the Asturian proletariat, fighting against superior forces, feeding the hungry masses, attempting to establish its stern discipline and order in the face of the bombardment and sabotage of the armies sent against them by the Lerroux-Robles reaction, aroused the admiration and respect even of its enemies in Asturias.

Instructions were issued by the Revolutionary Committee against all acts of pillage, with orders to arrest and shoot pillagers. All of the workers' parties and organisations were called to the central headquarters of the government to participate in the administration of the ruling Committee and to arrange for the defence of the Workers' and Peasants' Republic.

The Workers' Militia, though hastily assembled, was well organised and disciplined, consisting chiefly of the Asturian miners, soldiers, munitions-factory workers, and peasants. Leaders sprang from the ranks. A special corps of miners was organised to dynamite the troops sent against them. With the greatest daring and skill they carried out their work. As one Spanish correspondent put it, " They carried out their tasks with amazing efficiency and without the slightest regard for their own lives."

Another correspondent tells of the Workers' Militia marching into Oviedo: " I watched them march through. It was an indescribable spectacle. The first of the men carried baskets with self-manufactured hand-grenades. With the shout: ' Forward, comrades ! ' they charged into the withering fire of the Civil Guards, who were barricaded in the building of the telephone headquarters."

One doctor in Oviedo, who was impressed into the medical service of the Workers' Militia of Asturias, writing in the reactionary newspaper

Estampa of his experiences, tells of the undying heroism of the Asturian workers. The wounded began to pour into the hospitals. Workers badly injured were impatient at the delay of the doctors. They wanted to get back to the firing lines. The doctor tells of one fighter who was brought in:

" ' Patch me up quickly,' one wounded man demanded. 'Do me first, I want to get back. We must take Santa Clara barracks. It is full of Civil Guards.'

" ' You must go to bed,' the doctor ordered.

" The man refused to go to bed and went off without attention. The next day he was found dead in the roadway.

" A wounded man arrived, supported by a thin youngster with the face of a woman. He carried a rifle slung over his shoulder and bandoleers of cartridges. Turning to me, probably because I was nearest, he declared: ' It's terrible.' ' What's terrible ? ' I asked. ' Comrade Belarme has been shot. When he saw that we were not making as much progress as he would have liked at the prefecture, he dashed forward, without cover, to bomb the place, and they shot him down with a volley.' "

When the Asturian proletariat was finally defeated, the slaughter was frightful. Hundreds were massed against walls, men, women, and children, and mowed down with machine guns. The bodies of the dead and wounded were piled up and burned together.

Oviedo was subjected to a frightful bombardment from aeroplane and artillery. Yet, although the workers were trapped, their humanitarianism and consideration were described by an eye-witness, Hans Theodor Joel, writing in the *Neue Weltbühne*, the Prague German émigré weekly, as follows:

" The workers did not oppress the population, not even the middle classes. They did not commit murder and wholesale destruction, but helped all those who suffered from the fighting.

" Let me cite one example among thousands. When the grenades and aeroplane bombs of General Ochoa set fire to the lyceum in Oviedo that was being used as barracks and staff headquarters and there was danger that at any moment the more than two tons of dynamite stored there might explode and destroy that whole part of the city, the Red Guards not only warned the middle-class inhabitants of the district but helped them as best they could, while the fighting went forward, to get their property out of their threatened dwelling-place."

Provincial armed forces at the command of the government, even the regular army and navy, were either insufficient or unreliable for the task of smashing the Asturian uprising. The Lerroux-Robles government found it necessary for the first time in Spanish history to transport the Spanish Foreign Legion and Riff troops to the mainland to quell the Asturian workers. After fifteen days of fighting, during which the government freely employed bombing planes, laying a good part of Oviedo in ruins, the miners were finally subdued. A large number of them retreated into the hills.

With the defeat of the Catalan uprising, with the failure of the workers of Madrid to take the offensive *en masse*, the Asturian workers were left in the lurch.

In Catalonia the fighting was much more complicated, involving many diverse interests. Catalonia, it will be remembered, was the pretext for the crisis that led to the fall of the Samper government. The Supreme Court of Spain had nullified an Agrarian Reform Law benefiting the tenants and small landowners which had been passed by the Catalan government prior to October 1934. Catalonia, therefore, considered the Supreme Court action a further blow to the independence it had won as a result of the establishment of the 1931 Republic.

In opposition to the chauvinist fascist cliques in Madrid, there were in Catalonia a number of parties, working at cross purposes. The most important of them were: the bourgeois Left

national forces, under the leadership of Companys;
the anarcho-syndicalist C.N.T. and the F.A.I.,
by far the largest working-class organisations;
the Socialist Party; and the Communist Party.
While Luis Companys, president of the Catalan
Generalidad, proclaimed the independence of
Catalonia and was supported by more than eighty
per cent of the towns and villages in Catalonia,
he did not proceed to the arming of the workers
to defend that independence and to win their
own demands in the struggle against fascism.
At the same time the anarchists refused to participate in a joint movement with the Catalan
Left nationalist parties on the ground that it
was immaterial to them whether they were
ruled by the exploiters of Madrid or Barcelona,
whether the detested, oppressive State wore
the mask of democratic republic or fascist dictatorship. Differing little from this view was the small
but voluble Trotskyist band.

When the signal for resistance to Gil Robles
provocation in Madrid was sounded, Companys
wasted precious time manœuvring with General
Domingo Batet of the Catalan army garrison.
General Batet was invited to join the independent
movement. He requested one hour to make his
decision. Before the hour was past he gave his
emphatic reply by ordering his troops to fire. The
Barcelona workers, Socialists, Communists, and

young republicans, fought valiantly, but were decisively defeated on October 7, owing to the organised attack of Batet's troops, numbering more than ten thousand. The Catalan national government was forced to capitulate. The Madrid fascists breathed easier. They could now settle with brave little Asturias.

In Madrid the fighting, though fierce, was most sporadic. In working-class sections skirmishes immediately began between troops and workers. The workers in Madrid set up barricades and at first the troops could not cope with the workers' offensive. Fighting continued until October 12. But the lack of preparation for large-scale mass struggle was apparent. Above all, it was evident that there was no previous political stimulus to unite and to rally the workers and peasants for the assault. In Madrid the workers concentrated mostly against strike-breaking, whereas workers' special shock troops attempted to harry the government centres and picked troops. Workers with machine guns stormed the Cortes, the Bank of Spain, police headquarters, and the like. Fighting, however, was hindered by lack of weapons and by lack of organisation. Street fighting after a few days fell off to ineffectual sniping. At first the government was slow to take action against the workers. Great care was used to pick only the most trusted detachment of the army. A section of the

aviation troops encamped at the central aerodrome in Madrid refused to take part against
the workers.

The aftermath of the fall of Workers' and
Peasants' rule in Asturias was a terrible foretaste
of the terrorism the fascists were to show in the
July Civil War. Men, women and children were
mowed down by machine guns, their bodies piled
in a heap and burned. Working-class casualties
were everywhere extremely heavy. In Asturias
alone, the dead numbered between two and three
thousand. Throughout Spain, including Asturias,
the total was set at five to six thousand. Sixty
thousand persons were arrested and thirty
thousand finally condemned to terms of imprisonment varying from one year to life. The prisons
were bursting with men and women accused of
having participated in the uprising.

Subsequent developments and sober political
estimates of the October events revealed why the
uprising provoked by the fascists did not and could
not succeed. The chief lessons were: First, the lack
of necessary cohesion, the absence of unity among
the proletarian revolutionary parties. Second, the
adamant neutrality of the anarchists between what
they called the choice of two evils, the rule of
Madrid or Barcelona, the one fascist, the other
national revolutionary. Third, the peasantry was
not sufficiently won over to the side of the workers

against the fascist provocateurs. Fourth, the middle class was largely neglected and was allowed to remain neutral in the contest between the workers and the fascists. This mistake was one of the first remedied in the days after the defeat of the October uprising.

Though the military actions of the workers were decisively crushed, the most striking political phenomenon in Spain after the October events was lack of a defeatist spirit among the proletariat. The reverses and bitter experiences of the defeat served chiefly to spur them to further unity against their fascist enemies. Fascism was unable to take the fullest advantage of its victory. The workers' organisations, though illegal, remained intact, and even strengthened themselves, in contrast to the aftermath of the bloody February events in Austria in the same year, when Chancellor Engelbert Dollfuss gave fascism full sway by destroying the trade unions and the legal revolutionary workers' parties.

October 1934, with all its mistakes, lives in the consciousness of the Spanish working class as a promise of ultimate and complete emancipation.

CHAPTER VIII

THE INQUISITION REBORN

IF THE PERIOD of political and military preparations for the fascist coup of 1936 is to be traced to
its origin, the days of terror and revenge from the
defeat of the October uprising to the February
1936 election must be examined. With thirty
thousand Leftists in prison, the most important
leaders apprehended and facing trial, the reactionary parties saw their opportunity to mangle the
Republic and prepare for the final blow, even
if it meant civil war, to achieve fascism.

A dual course was followed. On the one hand,
ferocious terror was directed against the workers'
organisations and the Catalan nationalist Left.
Social legislation and agrarian reforms were
whittled away. And on the other hand, the Rights
acted to strengthen their grip on the machinery
of the Republic, to compose their own many
differences, to manœuvre the bourgeois Centre
either completely to their side or entirely out of
existence.

To curb the revolutionary temper of the

workers and peasants, heavy punishment was meted out to the prisoners of October. Martial law was enforced for five months. In the first two days after the declaration of martial law seven thousand more opponents of the Lerroux government were arrested.

The Oviedo miners, in the province of Asturias, bore the brunt of the terror. Government troops, particularly the hated Foreign Legion, shot seven hundred workers in the infantry garrison. Groups of suspected participants in the October uprising were shot down in the streets and in the public squares, as well as on the warships which had mutinied.

Executions of victims of the October defeat continued right on up until the February 1936 elections.

Manuel Azaña, Luis Companys, Largo Caballero, Teodomiro Menendez, Gonzalez Peña, were among the leading figures that were tried. The prisons were packed to the bursting-point. The Madrid penitentiary housed six thousand, with three and four in cells built for one. The toll of October was heavy enough, even if it were to sink into relative unimportance compared to that of the July Civil War. The most reliable figures tabulated the following: 60,000 to 80,000 prisoners; 5,000 dead; 10,000 wounded.

Torture was freely resorted to, especially in

Asturias. A protest petition, signed by 564 political prisoners in Oviedo, either condemned or awaiting trial, gave a graphic description of the cruelties they were subjected to. To the Public Prosecutor they declared:

" A modern inquisition has been set up: twisting of the scrotum, burning of the sex organs and other parts of the body, squeezing of the hands and toes with pincers; use of a torture chair; hitting the hands and knees with hammers; forcing toothpicks under the finger-nails, scalding with boiling water, pretending to execute prisoners, ordering prisoners to dig their own graves, beating of prisoners in the presence of their mothers, sisters, or wives."

Luis Companys and six other members of the Catalan Left were tried and condemned to thirty years' imprisonment for " inciting military rebellion." Companys insisted that he alone was responsible, but thirty years' imprisonment was the final word for *all*, without the right of appeal. Manuel Azaña was tried, hounded, and acquitted. Two Socialist deputies, Indalecio Prieto and Señorita Margarita Nelken, who fled to France after the October events, were also convicted.

A most sensational trial, because it so forcefully helped to defeat the Lerroux-Robles reactionary groups by the mass resentment it aroused, was that of Teodomiro Menendez and Gonzalez

Peña. They were accused of leading the Oviedo revolt. Though they were condemned to death, popular anger grew to the proportions of a mass movement that stayed the enforcement of the death sentences.

The fascist and reactionary groups began to quarrel among themselves over the extent of the terror. A latent crisis developed in the government, Gil Robles and the C.E.D.A. insisting on more terror, the Radicals fearing that more prison terms and executions would goad the people into new attempts at revolt.

Most interesting was the spirit among the peasantry and proletariat. The toiling population showed none of the signs of temporary defeat which dogged the Italian, German, and Austrian workers, in varying degrees, after the victory of fascism. True, fascism had not completely conquered in Spain, but the will and the plans were there. Discontent continued to seethe because economic conditions grew worse—and the fascists could neither curb nor destroy the workers' organisations despite the brutal terror. Trade unions and the Socialist and Communist parties actually grew under the terror, while the Anarcho-Syndicalist and Anarchist organisations lost some influence because of their " neutral " policy in the fighting.

An interesting political development went on

in the prisons where Socialists, Communists and Anarcho-Syndicalists were cooped up together in a manner they had never before experienced. The jails were turned into breeding-grounds of proletarian unity and schools for drawing lessons from the failure of the uprising. United Front committees were organised in the prisons. The prisoners refused to deal with the prison authorities except through their elected committees. Marxist libraries were installed. It was in prison that Largo Caballero arrived at the firm conclusion that Communist and Socialist unity was an urgent necessity.

Although revolutionary publications were suppressed after the October uprising (with the exception of the anarcho-syndicalist *Solidaridad Obrera* and the anarchist *Tierra y Libertad*) a widespread and successful movement for the legality of the workers' organisations sprang up. It was not, however, until May 26, 1935 that the police authorities permitted the opening of the Socialist headquarters, in Madrid, Seville, Huelva, and other important cities.

After October there was complete working unanimity between Lerroux and Gil Robles. Lerroux even referred to Robles as his successor. It was obvious that the Robles-Sotelo brain trust was running the country and that Lerroux was taking orders.

The October 4 government leaned heavily on the Right, with support from the Centre. In other words, it was a government under a Republic which, in its majority, was openly and irreconcilably opposed to any republic.

The Rights, in control of the government, began systematically to destroy the gains of the 1931 Republic. The agrarian reforms were wiped out. Socialist and Communist municipal councillors were ousted, and reactionaries appointed in their stead. The Church was strengthened, and its bond with the State re-established. The autonomy granted Catalonia and Biscay under the Constitution was curbed.

However, the attempted fascist bloc after the October defeat was characterised by its inability to come to an agreement for the formation of a strong, dictatorial government. A series of Cabinet crises and the resignation of ministers, marked its course. The Socialists had voted against returning to the Cortes. Gil Robles decided on a policy of sniping to drive out of the Cabinet those ministers whom he considered obstacles in the march to fascism. On November 17, 1934 Foreign Minister Samper and Minister of War Hidalgo were forced to resign.

With the resignation of Hidalgo and Samper, Robles had won his first victory over the leaders of the Radical Party. He followed up his advantage

Gs

by forcing the resignation of the Minister of Education, Villalobos, a Liberal Democrat. As Minister of Education, Villalobos was too " secular " for the Jesuit Robles. José Martinez de Velasco of the Agrarian Party, Minister of Agriculture, was next to tender his resignation. Velasco resigned for Rightist causes: he regarded the government policy as too charitable to the prisoners of October.

On March 29, 1935 the Lerroux-Robles Cabinet resigned as a result of the Catholic and Agrarian opposition to the commutation of the death sentence imposed on Peña and Menendez. This was the fifth crisis since the Cabinet assumed office in October 1934. The chief bone of contention was the extent of the terror and the degree of fascism to be employed against the revolutionary proletariat. The C.E.D.A., the Agrarians, and the Liberal Democrats desired to go the limit. The Radicals spoke for leniency because their own party members, closer to public opinion, feared the consequences of unbridled fascist terror. The crucial moment arose when Gonzalez Peña and nineteen others were condemned to death.

On May 6, 1935 Lerroux formed a new Cabinet, including five members of the Popular Action, with Gil Robles in the ominous position of Minister of War. During this period after October the C.E.D.A. had adopted a clear-cut policy. Their main aim was to protect the interests of the big capitalists and the large landowners, in conjunction with the Agrarian Party. Inasmuch as the C.E.D.A. was decidedly fascist, but without a fascist mass storm-troop and in an exclusively Catholic country, it resorted to the most seductive Catholic demagogy. It appealed especially to the poor peasants and the unemployed. It hoped to create a mass proletarian base for its reactionary aims. A paternalistic unemployment programme was proposed; even a few large estates were seized (with adequate compensation for their owners) upon which to settle small groups of peasants.

As Minister of War, Gil Robles was an active man. Only his closest confidants knew why at the time. He ordered war manœuvres in Asturias under his personal supervision. On July 1, 1935 he was openly accused of reorganising the army for the purpose of a *coup d'État*. Señor Robles hotly denied the charge. If he were going to make a coup, he boasted, he would not need the army: the people would be with him. Manœuvres in the Guadarrama mountains during his incumbency cost the Republic dearly in 1936. It was under his administration in 1935 that cement entrenchments were built for the fascists in 1936.

Along with the internal revival of military ardour, Gil Robles devised plans for increasing the fortifications of the Balearic Islands.

Having prepared the army, Gil Robles and his associates planned to revise the Constitution before the end of the year. Parliament was then to vote to dissolve itself. New elections were planned, which the Right felt sure they would win. The army would help the legal authorities do the rest. Lerroux's new government lasted only a few months. The Agrarians, dissatisfied with the policies of the Lerroux Cabinet, and the consolidation of five Cabinet posts into one, and further objecting to the transfer from Catalonia to Madrid of public service works, hastened the resignation of Lerroux and his Right coalition Cabinet.

The next Cabinet was headed by Joaquin Chapaprieta. For Gil Robles and Calvo Sotelo it was another step in the journey to fascism. Under the pretext of economy, the number of ministers was reduced from twelve to nine. Gil Robles retained the post of Minister of War. He had not yet finished his preparations for civil war when that exigency arose. Alejandro Lerroux accepted the portfolio of the Foreign Ministry on the plea of President Alcalá-Zamora that an experienced man was needed in view of the Ethiopian war. The Left insisted on the dissolution of Parliament and the holding of new elections because of the permanent government crisis.

By the latter part of October the Chapaprieta Cabinet had been exposed in a nasty graft scandal.

Daniel Straus, a Mexican citizen, made a formal complaint to Premier Chapaprieta that he had paid two million pesetas to a Cabinet Minister, to certain unnamed Rightist deputies, and to other government officials, for a gambling concession in San Sebastián. Under the Republican-Socialist government gambling had been outlawed in Spain. Chapaprieta withheld the details of the scandal from the public on the ground that they were subject to investigation by the Attorney-General.

More unsavoury to the peasant masses than the little-understood scandals was the crude modification of the agrarian laws favouring the wealthy landlords, railroaded through the Cortes. The law was demagogically held up as a boon to the peasants. They were to get the land, and the bereft landlords a guarantee of adequate compensation. The injured landlords were to be paid out of a sinking fund, with assurance to four per cent interest until final settlement was made. So favourable was this scheme for the landlords that one member of the Cortes remarked: " Landowners will now line up in long queues to have their estates expropriated."

To cap the terror after October 1934, Spain was being driven towards an economic catastrophe. The basic labour laws passed in 1932 were destroyed. Wages of urban workers had been reduced from ten and twelve pesetas to four and

five. Wages of agricultural workers had been
lowered from eight and nine pesetas to one and
a half for men and sixty centimos for women for
a workday lasting from sun-up to sunset.
Discriminatory laws were passed against the small
peasantry.

Millions had been voted to the clergy, the railway companies, the army, the Civil Guard, and
the police. Official figures set the jobless in Spain
at 536,000 in 1933 and 780,242 in 1935. It was
unofficially estimated that the out-of-work numbered about 1,500,000. While the number of
unemployed was increasing, the budget for public
works was cut in 1935 to 628,000,000 pesetas: it
had been 873,000,000 in 1933.

National economy was virtually ruined by the
parties of the Right. While the rest of the world
showed some economic improvement in 1935,
Spain, under the rule of the C.E.D.A. and the
Centrists, recorded a substantial decline in production and foreign trade. Spanish exports dropped
from 1,548,424,000 pesetas in 1933 to 1,393,370,000
pesetas in 1935, reversing the general world trend.

Besides the difficulties encountered within the
government itself, it confronted growing opposition of the workers, the peasants, and a serious
People's Front movement uniting the radicalised
middle class and republicans with the Socialist
and Communist united front. With the Centre

becoming identified with the C.E.D.A. policies in the coalition government, the Left Republicans, under the leadership of Manuel Azaña, showed a remarkable growth of strength after the October uprising.

For the middle class, the Left Republican Party was the logical channel for the expression of their anti-fascist indignation. The prosecution of Azaña, the outstanding figure among the Spanish republicans, rallied all anti-fascists to his defence. Driven underground, denied meeting-privileges, persecuted, the workers also were able to express themselves legally through the mass meetings organised by the Left Republicans for Azaña. However, this was not only an expedient but an outgrowth of the People's Front policy of greater unity around the central issue of stopping the terror, defeating fascism, and saving the Republic as the best means of future progress in Spain. The Republican opposition, too, had returned to the Cortes and was the general spokesman for the anti-fascist front.

The fateful year 1936 opened with an attempt to bend before the oncoming storm by the ruse of retaining the reactionary set-up by a shift to a conservative republican and Centre combination. An appeal was made through the Centre to win the waning allegiance of the middle class. When Gil Robles thought the time had come for him to take over the exclusive receivership of the Republic, critical differences arose. President Alcalá-Zamora did not believe the time had come to transform the Republic directly into a fascist dictatorship. The Cortes, therefore, was dissolved on January 7 and elections set for February 16 and March 1.

Actually there was one issue dominating in the campaign: the Republic *versus* Fascism.

CHAPTER IX

THE PEOPLE'S FRONT

THE OCTOBER UPRISING and setback forced much suffering upon the Spanish people, and especially the working class, but it also gave them a fighting weapon for their next trial of strength. That weapon was unity. For many years the monarchy had maintained itself despite all corruption and decay mainly because its opponents expended a considerable amount of their energy fighting among themselves. The reactionaries under the Republic were somewhat less fortunate.

The first step to unify the progressive elements in the country had been taken on August 17, 1930, when the so-called Pact of San Sebastián was signed by all the republican factions, including the Socialists. This pact provided for a common front against the monarchy and little else. No doubt it was one of the most important factors making for the overthrow of the monarchy, which occurred the very next year.

But the limitations of the Pact of San Sebastián were very great. It was completely negative in conception with the exception of the planks promising religious freedom and some vague measure of autonomy for Catalonia. The pact completely subordinated the Socialists to the most timid and wavering middle-class republicans, including such stalwart conservatives as Lerroux, Miguel Maura, and Alcalá-Zamora. There was nothing resembling a fair division of authority and responsibility between the middle class and the labour republicans.

As a result, the Pact of San Sebastián died with the monarchy. The Socialist members of the first republican government supplied the fig-leaf needed by the republicans. It was Largo Caballero, then Minister of Labour, who gave this function a formulation in the spring of 1931 with the following words:

" I received an influential delegation of the Barcelona industrialists and of the representatives of the Spanish Chamber of Commerce, who expressed to me their fears regarding the selfish action of certain sections of the working class. In Catalonia, in particular, demands were made in a very forcible manner. The delegation requested the government to adopt energetic measures in order to meet this action of the workers.

" I replied that in my eyes such action was just as unpatriotic as the migration of those who take their capital with them in order to boycott Spain.

These two movements which cause great damage to our new system cannot be tolerated.

" The working class, which cannot abandon its demands once the Republic has been firmly established, must in the meantime consent to a truce."

This truce was concluded, however, at the expense of unity within the working class. The gap between the Socialists, Communists, and anarchists was not appreciably lessened in these first two years of the Republic. The conflict between the Socialist-led U.G.T. and the syndicalist C.N.T. continued unabated. Meanwhile reaction in the form of Gil Robles's Popular Action Party and the C.E.D.A. mended its political fences and plotted a come-back.

Beginning with the end of 1933, the Communists began to issue periodic appeals to the Socialists for a united front against the Lerroux government. But they were refused in every case. It was at this time that Largo Caballero began to shift his position and to make continuous progress towards a revolutionary Socialist policy, including united action with the Communists. But he was in the minority during those 1933 days and the Socialist leaders to the right of him, Indalecio Prieto and Julian Besteiro, were adamantine against any common action with either the Communists or the anarchists.

The united-front agitation of the Communists began to make headway only after the Republican-Socialist electoral defeat at the end of 1933. This progress was mainly among the rank and file of the Socialist Party and it was limited to certain localities. In 1934, Communists and Socialists began to co-operate in a number of strikes and demonstrations.

In the summer of 1934, Joaquin Maurin, who had previously been expelled from the Communist Party for " Right deviations," started agitation for Workers' Alliances in somewhat vague fashion. The Socialist Party co-operated with Maurin and adopted the Alliances as model organisations for the whole of Spain. In the beginning the Communists bitterly criticised both Maurin and the Socialist leaders for their conception of the Alliances and refused to enter them.

The Communist criticism turned mainly on the point that the Workers' Alliances were conceived solely as linking committees between the constituent organisations instead of as mass organisations democratically elected in the factories and farms. The Socialists conceived of the Alliances as a general staff reserved for the day of the revolution instead of as a fighting medium, not only for the future but for the day-to-day struggles of the peasant. Equally important in the Communist indictment was the fact that the Alliances completely omitted the peasants from the scope of their activity. In a predominantly agrarian country, they considered this hardly tenable and raised the alternative of Workers' and Peasants' Alliances.

Later the Communists regretted that they had boycotted the Alliances instead of having immediately joined them and tried to transform them. On September 23, 1934, however, the Communists changed their tactics and joined the Alliances, although they did not withdraw their criticisms. Barely two weeks later, the uprising broke out in Catalonia, Asturias, and elsewhere in the north. Officially, the uprising was supposed to be under the leadership of the Alliances. In actual fact, they failed to function, except in the Asturias. Basically, the failure of the Alliances to lead the uprising to victory was due to the fact that even on the eve of the revolt neither the Socialist, Communist, or syndicalist trade unions nor the peasants, unemployed, and soldiers belonged—or could belong—to the Alliances. This was their fatal defect.

Just about this time the idea of a People's Front began to take form in France, where the Communists and Socialists had already been united by a pact signed on July 27, 1934. At a congress of the French Radical-Socialist Party, held in Nantes on October 24, 1934, Maurice Thorez, the general secretary of the French Communist Party, formulated the idea of a People's Front. This People's Front, according to Thorez, would embrace all progressive elements among the workers, farmers, and middle class for a militant fight against fascism and to better the working- and living-conditions of the working people. While none of the participating organisations in the People's Front would surrender their independent activity and programme, all would co-operate against the common foe. It was made explicit that the People's Front would not be commissioned or expected to introduce revolutionary changes—the Communists considered only a Soviet revolution could do that—but that it would simultaneously repulse the threat of fascism, improve living- and working-conditions, and prepare the way for an even higher stage of class struggle which would lead to Socialism.

Events in France soon had their repercussions in Spain, and the Spanish Communists began to agitate for the formation of a Spanish People's Front against the danger of fascism represented not only by the Lerroux-Robles government but by the Falange Española of José Primo de Rivera, the Renovación Española of Goicoechea and Gil Robles's C.E.D.A. When the French People's Front pact was signed on July 14, 1935, it aided the Spanish campaign immeasurably.

Just as the Communists and Socialists had joined in united-front actions in September 1934, immediately prior to the October uprising, so the Spanish People's Front was finally achieved just prior to another critical moment—the February 16, 1936 election. The People's Front took longer to become established in Spain than in France, but it was no less effective.

On January 16, 1936—just one month before the election—a pact of common action was signed by the Communist Party, the Socialist Party, Azaña's Left Republican Party, Martínez Barrios's Republican Union, Companys's Catalonian Left Party and the Nin-Maurin Partido Obrero de Unificación Marxista (Workers' Party of Marxian Unity—P.O.U.M.). This last party, relatively small in numbers and localised in Catalonia, had just been formed by a coalition of the followers of Maurin and Andrés Nin, a follower of Leon Trotsky, who had fallen out of grace with Trotsky because he refused to disband and join the Socialists according to Trotsky's instructions. It soon left the People's Front and began to lay down a violent barrage against the whole policy.

The People's Front Pact was divided into eight sections, and almost all represented some degree of compromise and concession by all the signatories. In general, it was not at all as radical and satisfactory to the Left elements as was the French People's Front Pact.

The first section provided for a broad amnesty for all political prisoners committed to jail for opposition activity since November 1933. The number of prisoners was estimated at thirty thousand—perhaps the largest in Europe except in Germany and Italy. It also stated that all public officials and workers in public or private enterprises dismissed from their positions for political reasons, or following strikes of a political nature, were to be immediately reinstated.

The second section promised to reform the courts in order to reinforce the constitutional guarantees of the Republic, to reform the Cortes and provincial and municipal laws, safeguard private security against arbitrary arrest, humanise the prison regime, and open an inquiry into abuses committed by the police and the armed forces.

The third section promised the peasants reduction in taxes and in excessive rents or leases, an increase in farm credits, revalorisation of agricultural products, and a new tenancy law. The fourth section provided for the protection of small industry and trading. The fifth, devoted to unemployment, pledged a vast programme of public works. The sixth, dealing with currency and finance, promised regulations for private banking, modification of the system of direct taxes, and the reform of credit through the Bank of Spain. The seventh section provided for the re-establishment of labour legislation, minimum wages, and State direction and unification of private charities. The eighth part, dealing with education, promised schools, professional education, and greater access to secondary higher education for the working-class students. Finally, the pact stated that the international policy of Spain would conform to the principles and methods of the League of Nations.

This pact was in no sense revolutionary. In many respects it did not live up to the expectations of the labour signatories. It was definitely pro-gressive, however, and constituted a definite basis for co-operation among all the progressive forces in the forthcoming election. If the People's Front won the election, the labour groups recog-nised that the pact would liberate those thousands of political prisoners who would give new life, new strength, and new inspiration to their struggle. The pact itself could later be revised as the demands of experience indicated.

Meanwhile, having unified their forces—with the exception of the anarchists and the P.O.U.M. —the defenders of the Republic were ready to engage in the February electoral battle, which promised to be their liberation or their doom.

Hs

CHAPTER X

VICTORY AND INTRIGUES

FEBRUARY 16, 1936 was the most fateful election day in Spanish history. The People's Front landslide had a shattering effect on the hopes of the fascists. It was on that day that the fascists, monarchists, and other conservative enemies of the democratic Republic saw their carefully laid plans for the utilisation of the Republic snowed under by an avalanche of anti-fascist votes. They never expected so overwhelming a victory for the People's Front. At worst, they looked for a stalemate. Such an eventuality, they believed, would present the Cortes with an irreconcilable division, rendering Parliament worthless as an instrument of action. Were such the case, the issue of power would be thrown to the army. That would have satisfied the fascists.

Discontent with the Rightists, fear and distrust of fascist manœuvres, anger over the persecution of the October 1934 victims, disappointment with the demagogy of the C.E.D.A., gathered from many streams into the one raging torrent of the People's Front and wiped away the reactionary grip on the Cortes. The People's Front triumphed throughout Spain. The coalition of the Rights which led to the November 1933 victory was now countered by a more smashing sweep of the Left by the concentration of the People's Front. The more reactionary the individual leaders, the greater their personal defeat in the elections. No election in Spanish history had ever been so important. Its aftermath was to shake the world.

The People's Front this time, in its energetic election campaign, successfully persuaded many anarcho-syndicalists to vote, a procedure formerly anathema to them. The Workers' Alliance had begun to unite the Communists, Socialists, and syndicalists. The united proletarian front, soon to prove itself still hardier in the fires of civil war, was embraced in the broader People's Front consisting of Communists, Socialists, the supporters of the Left Republicans, the Republican Union of Martínez Barrios, the Azaña Left Republicans and Companys's Catalan Left Nationalists.

Detailed figures of this fateful election are of value not only to record the gains made by the People's Front, but to illuminate the issues of the Civil War. Of a total of 473 seats in the Cortes, the parties of the People's Front won the clear majority of 268. The Right, Centre,

and outright fascist parties lost 147 seats. Spain
had overwhelmingly put its trust of democracy
and progress in the hands of the People's Front.

The final tabulation of the election results
showed the complexion of the Cortes to be as
follows:

PEOPLE'S FRONT	1936	1933	gains
Left-Republican parties	158	62	96
Workers' parties	110	59	51
Total	268	121	147

CENTRE AND RIGHT			losses
Centre	48	139	91
Right parties	157	213	56
Total	205	352	147

According to the composition of the most important parties, the changes were as follows:

PEOPLE'S FRONT	1936	1933	gain or loss
Left Republicans (Azaña's party)	81	7	+74
Republican Union (Martínez Barrios's party)	36	23	+13
Esquerra (Left Republicans of Catalonia)	29	23	+ 6
Socialist Party	98	58	+40
Communist Party	16	1	+15
Other Left parties	18	9	+ 9

CENTRE AND RIGHT	1936	1933	gain or loss
Radical Party (Lerroux's party)	8	80	—72
C.E.D.A. (Gil Robles's party)	94	113	—19
Agrarian Party	13	39	—26
Liberal-Democrat Party	1	9	— 8
Lliga (Catalan Right)	11	23	—12
Conservative Party	3	18	—15
Monarchist parties	24	32	— 8
Other parties of Centre and Right	51	38	+13

Popular participation in the election was greater than in 1933. For example, in Madrid as against 75·02 per cent of the eligible voters who cast ballots in the 1933 elections, 77·48 per cent voted in the February 1936 elections. The figures in other leading cities were: Barcelona, 1933, 60·15 per cent, 1935, 69 per cent (the especially low figure of Barcelona is due to anarcho-syndicalist abstention, and the rise in 1936 is accounted for by a change in the anarcho-syndicalist attitude towards voting); Badajoz, 1933, 74 per cent, 1936, 75 per cent; Malaga, 1933, 51·76 per cent, 1936, 80 per cent.

The People of Spain had spoken.

Bitterly the fascists and monarchists assailed the election results. Gil Robles in *El Debate* declared: " The issue was one of revolution against law and order, respect for religion, property, the family, and national unity, with socialism the real enemy."

Democratic victories democratically carried out were considered " revolution " by the upholders of Spain's ancient shame. José Calvo Sotelo, monarchist, had put the issue a little more bluntly just prior to the voting. " Democracy in Spain," he declared, " will always lead inevitably to Communism." Therefore democracy must be destroyed.

When democracy gave the electoral victory to the People's Front, the fascists had only one way to " correct " the will of the people, and that was by their old and tried methods—suppression, terror, bloodshed. The Republic, born in such gaiety of spirit, so happy over the departure of the King, so joyful over its present electoral victory, hesitated to believe the worst of the reactionaries.

The first thought of the people after the electoral victory was to open the hated bastilles where thirty thousand of their brothers, sisters, sons, daughters, friends, and comrades had been incarcerated since the October 1934 uprising. Impatience broke all bounds. Some of the prisons were stormed and the occupants set free. The people were beside themselves in their haste to liberate the victims of the Lerroux-Robles terror, whose crime had been to seek the end of feudal-monarchist-fascist domination. The government quickly released thirty thousand prisoners. It followed that up with the rapid reinstatement of thousands of workers and agricultural labourers who had been thrown out on the streets on account of their activities in October 1934.

The victory of the Cortes could not be considered complete with Alcalá-Zamora remaining as President of Spain. He was looked upon by the majority of the Spanish people as the chief accomplice of the assassins of the Asturian workers, as a pliable agent of Gil Robles and Lerroux. On April 7, 1936 debate was opened for the removal of President Alcalá-Zamora. Indalecio Prieto, right-wing Socialist, spoke for the majority group. Lawyer-like, he outlined Alcalá-Zamora's crimes. His continuation as President of the Republic, Prieto exclaimed, was inconsistent with the sovereign will of the people as expressed in the February elections. Gil Robles defended Alcalá-Zamora. Like a skilful Jesuit, Gil Robles in his defence of Alcalá-Zamora appealed to the republicans, appealed to them to split from the Socialists and Communists. That was the greater condemnation in the eyes of the People's Front. The Communist deputies called Alcalá-Zamora a murderer and shouted: " Imprison him for his crimes in Asturias."

The vote to oust Alcalá-Zamora was 238 ayes and 5 nocs; the rest abstained: 209 votes were required to dismiss the President. Diego Martínez

Barrios, President of the Cortes, automatically became President until the next elections.

In the April 26 election for representatives to meet with the Cortes for the election of a President, the monarchists and fascists abstained from voting. The People's Front won an overwhelming victory. On May 10 Manuel Azaña, the only candidate, was elected by the People's Front as second President of the Second Republic.

Aware of the strenuous efforts that the Rightists would make to break the People's Front alliance between the Left Republicans and the proletarian parties of the united front, the Socialist and Communist parties lost no opportunity of making clear their position towards the Azaña government. Each in its own way, yet acting more unitedly as conditions became more strained owing to fascist sabotage and constant rioting, sought to prevent a rupture in the ranks of the People's Front.

The Rightist parties preyed on the fears of Azaña and his followers—more particularly those among the People's Front adherents even to the right of Azaña—and harped on the idea that the proletariat, having won the election with the help of the republicans, would now betray its ally and march over its body to the Socialist revolution, to Bolshevism.

To scotch such arguments, *Claridad*, organ of

the Left Socialists, very soon after the election, voicing the stand of Largo Caballero and the overwhelming majority of his party, declared:

" We shall be on the side of the government in order to help it carry out the joint programme with all the necessary determination, even if this programme does not satisfy us entirely. We will, however, not give the government our unreserved confidence as we did from 1931 to 1933. The lesson was too hard and we will not renounce our right to criticise in order to maintain the vigilance of the working class, which is now marching forward to the final goal of our class, and, at the slightest sign of weakening, to set the working class itself against its present allies."

José Diaz, general secretary of the Communist Party, deputy for Madrid, issued the following statement virtually to the same effect, when the People's Front victory was reported:

" The People's Front must not be disbanded. On the contrary, it must be strengthened and given every possible activity. We believe it is necessary to continue the action jointly—Communists, Socialists, and Anarchists—firmly united in the Workers' and Peasants' Alliances, in conjunction with the Left Republican and democratic masses. This will be the best guarantee that the bourgeois-democratic revolution will be realised in its final implications."

Even leaders to the right of President Azaña in the People's Front were enthusiastic and hopeful over the achievements of the revivified Republic. For example, Martínez Barrios at the Republican Union Congress in the latter part of June 1936 could make this summary of accomplishment and the necessity for maintaining the people's unity against fascist provocations:

"We triumphed in February," he said, "and again took charge of the destinies of the Republic. Three facts stand out since then: first, the fulfilment of the obligations of the People's Front Pact; second, the dismissal of the first President of the Republic; and, third, the present situation in Spain. Let us examine the three.

"Since February 16 we have accomplished the following: amnesty, replacement of discharged workers, draft of reform of the Guaranty Tribunal, reform of the law of public order, reform of the judiciary, etc.

"Few governments could present so well fulfilled a list of realisations of what they had promised. My testimony, not tinged by personal involvement in ministerial tasks, is impartial. But not alone for the fulfilment of the People's Front Pact should we urge a quickening of the pace.

"When these tasks are completed, should the parties of the People's Front separate? A grave responsibility rests in that answer. For me and the

Republican Union there is no choice; while the factions fighting against the regime continue to direct their attacks against the Republic, the People's Front must be maintained.

" The People's Front Pact imposes on the republican parties the obligation of retaining power jointly as originally agreed. There is a possibility of changing this clause. But how shall it be done ? It cannot be by replacing republican policy. Permit me to say at the same time that we do not repudiate amplification of the programme of the People's Front; neither do we refuse to discuss the hypothesis that the socialist forces, in union with the republicans, should hold power.

" A few final words to those who have special duties in the discipline of the parties. Do not desert your posts of vigilance in the towns assigned to you. This is imposed upon you not only by your ideas, but for the health of the fatherland."

A more detailed list of the accomplishments of the February victory and the backing of the Republic by the People's Front, as outlined by the proletarian parties, is the following :

1. Reinstatement of those discharged for political activity after January 1, 1934, with provision for compensation ranging from three to six month's wages.

2. General amnesty for those arrested as a result of the October 1934 events.

3. Semi-autonomous status of Catalonia regained; autonomy promised to Biscay.

4. Land provided to 87,000 peasants. Together with their families this included 500,000 people. Peasants who were expelled from their land were reinstated.

5. Restoration of the social legislation of the first period of the Republic.

6. Disbandment of some of the smaller fascist groups.

7. Some of the police forces purged of fascists.

8. A commission set up to fix the blame for the October murders, repressions, imprisonments, and tortures.

Within the ranks of the working-class parties and trade unions a two-sided process was going on. Above all, unity was growing. At the same time efforts were being exerted to engender splits; to provoke diversive strikes; to block that unification which would give labour greater unity.

Foremost was the unity achieved after February 16 between the Socialist-led and the Communist-led trade unions, and between the Socialist and Communist youth organisations. Progress had also been made towards organic unity of the Socialist and Communist parties—that is, their fusion into one party.

When the Unitary General Confederation of Labour (C.G.T.U.)—Communist—united with the General Workers' Union (U.G.T.)—Socialist—the consolidated union grew far beyond the combined strength of both. In June the U.G.T., as the united body was called, had in its ranks 940,000 industrial workers and 260,000 agricultural workers.

Still left outside was the powerful C.N.T. (National Confederation of Labour)—Anarchist—which spurned unity on the trade-union field, but could not simply reject the idea of working-class solidarity. The 1936 Congress of the C.N.T. therefore placed as a condition of unity the creation of new Alliances, after the Socialists and Communists had broken with the People's Front. The Socialists and Communists saw in this not only a dangerous bid to split the unity with the Left Republicans—wished for by the fascists—but an anarchist rejection of trade-union unity.

Meanwhile the Madrid organisation of the Socialist Party, headed by Largo Caballero, had passed a resolution, to be introduced at the next Socialist national congress, urging organic unity with the Communist Party, and a serious split threatened within the Socialist leadership.

Indalecio Prieto, the right-wing Socialist leader,

manœuvred to oust Largo Caballero, who undoubtedly had the support of the majority of
Socialists, as the events of the Civil War proved
later. This alarming danger of a Socialist split, the
tense situation created later on by fascist provocations in the great wave of strikes, and the clash
between the anarcho-syndicalists and the united
U.G.T. were grist to the fascist mill.

Mundo Obrero, Communist official organ, worried
over efforts of the fascists, Trotskyists, and some
anarcho-syndicalists to rupture the People's Front,
warned that under no circumstances must the
united action of Left Republicans and the proletarian parties be broken.[1]

Spanish fascism cast a long black shadow of the
coming of civil war well before its outbreak. A
very short time after the election the fascists got
over their dismay. Despite so overwhelming a
victory of the people, despite the toilers' determination to win economically what they had
ensured politically, the fascists showed a surprising
provocative boldness.

At first, in reply to the electoral victory of the
People's Front, the wealthy classes resorted to

[1] *La Batalla*, Trotskyist organ in Barcelona, after sharply criticising the
People's Front in January, when the P.O.U.M. withdrew, nevertheless
urged its followers to vote for the People's Front candidates. Yet the
burden of its policy thereafter was that the sooner the People's Front was
ended, the quicker the proletariat would get its due. Objectively, this was
ideologic aid to Rightists, whose greatest hope was to force just such a split
before they began their coup.

probably the most concerted economic sabotage that any country ever witnessed. Capital was exported by the hundreds of millions of pesetas. To force the peseta down on the world exchange, heavy withdrawals were made from banks, gold was shipped out of the country, and other usual methods of manipulating the currency were used. Business was deliberately slowed up. Even big landowners threatened sabotage by refusing to cultivate huge tracts. They declared that it would not be profitable to plant with farm wages rising and peasant agitation for land-distribution threatening their ownership of the crop.

On April 18, Gil Robles, Calvo Sotelo, and Juan Ventosa jointly warned Azaña that it was necessary to save the country from Bolshevism and chaos. They added threateningly that there would be no hope of economic improvement while " law and order " were threatened in Spain.

Azaña, answering the critics from the Right who aimed to have him split with the Left proletarian parties, declared: " There is no danger of waking up one morning and finding Communism ruling our country. There is a great need for social justice in Spain, and my purpose is to prevent the accumulation of great wealth by a few individuals while many suffer from hunger and poverty."

What the fascists particularly objected to was the fact that the Spanish workers (very much like the

French workers in June after the inauguration of the Blum government, though not with the same organisation and thoroughness) were forcing rapid improvements of their living-conditions, and the peasants were directly striving to settle the land question.

March was marked by murders, rioting, and other palpable signs that the fascists were not ready to accept as final the electoral decision of the people, nor the subsequent acts of the workers and peasants. On March 12, 1936 the companion and bodyguard of the prominent Socialist deputy Luis Jiminez Asuá was shot dead when fascists attempted to assassinate Jiminez Asuá himself. Using American gangster methods, five men opened a fusillade at the pair from a speeding car. The American gunman style became popular among the fascists, who, well supplied with money, cars, and machine guns, could easily keep the turmoil going and spread the feeling that the People's Front government could not maintain order.

As early as April, rumours grew louder that a military coup was under way and that a military dictatorship similar to that of the Primo de Rivera days was about to be established by the officers of the army. On the eve of the fifth anniversary of the Republic, April 14, 1936, Magistrate Manuel Pedregal was shot and killed by fascists. His crime, in their estimate, was the fact that he presided at the trial of six fascists convicted for the attempted murder of the Socialist deputy Luis Jiminez Asuá. In reprisal, fascist headquarters were stormed and their occupants killed or injured. Churches, suspected of caching arms, were broken into and sometimes burned.

As early as April 4, 1936 *Mundo Obrero* published a resolution of policy of the Communist Party towards the Azaña government and warned against the danger of fascism, " which is preparing to strike a blow by force with a view to establishing a bloody dictatorship. This raises before us the imperious need of strengthening and broadening the Workers' and Peasants' Militias, making them broad, self-defence organisations of a popular type."

José Diaz, Communist Party secretary, in a speech at Cartagena on April 9, declared : " Now you see why the C.E.D.A. makes the gesture of retiring from Parliament. Do you know why ? Because it is to facilitate its conspiracy with the barracks, where you will find many enemies of the Republic ; because it conspires with officials of the Civil Guard ; because it conspires in the casinos and in the boudoirs of the señoritas. In all of those places you will find many weapons. It will be necessary to eliminate them and to act before it is too late ! "

Is

The Communist Party sharply criticised President Azaña and Prime Minister Casares Quiroga for the government's dangerously slow response to the mounting evidence of the oncoming coup. It was pointed out that fascist officers in the army, members of the Falange Española, and the C.E.D.A., who were dismissed from their posts in the peninsula, were sent to Morocco, at higher pay. The Riff is a fascist recruiting centre, warned Socialists and Communists. Gil Robles was making frequent mysterious trips to France; " pleasure voyages," he called them. Actually he was conferring with Juan March, financier of the fascist Civil War, and King Alfonso. A few days before his death Calvo Sotelo stated that fascism would be the midwife of the monarchy in Spain.

La Politica, Azaña's newspaper, warned the Rightists that their provocations were exceeding all bounds. " Henceforth," it said, " we shall be guided by the instincts of self-preservation."

A Workers' Defence Militia was organised against the mounting fascist assaults. The purpose of the militia was to assist the governmental authorities to maintain the public peace. Militiamen were stationed at the approaches to Madrid. They searched cars for weapons. At night they examined documents of suspicious pedestrians. A well-disciplined force, they co-operated with the government to keep order. Included in the militia were Left Republican youth, peasants, Communists, Socialists, and members of the Estat Catala (a national revolutionary party of Catalonia).

Rioting, armed clashes, fascist provocations, strikes, land-seizures, bombings, assassinations, economic sabotage, and stubborn resistance by the wealthy industrialists and landed aristocracy continued ominously. By a thousand disruptive demonstrations, from lock-outs to officers' mutiny in the army, the opponents of the government served notice that they would not allow the Republic to proceed with its work of carrying through the programme of the People's Front. The fascists and other conservatives correctly feared that a small breach in the feudal dike would unloose a flood of revolutionary measures.

Opponents of the democratic Republic could boast superiority in arms. The number of dead in the street clashes were about equal on both sides. In an effort to curb the fascists, the government had ordered the arrest of the more slavish imitator of Hitler, José Antonio Primo de Rivera. Together with eight members of the Spanish Phalanx, Primo de Rivera was arrested, and his organisation dissolved. The Azaña government, however, instead of imprisoning Primo de Rivera for the crime of treason to the Republic, gave him a lighter sentence on the charge of " disturbing the peace."

Two months before the outbreak of the civil war, an incident occurred at Alcalá de Henares barracks, just outside of Madrid, that should have sufficiently warned the government. On May 18, following a scuffle between cavalry officers and workers, Premier Casares Quiroga decided to transfer two of the regiments. Officers of the two regiments mutinied against the order to remove the regiments to Valencia and Salamanca. Immediately sixty-two commissioned and non-commissioned officers were arrested and the mutiny quelled. But this definite symptom of unrest at the top of the army so near Madrid was not sufficiently heeded.

By the middle of June it became clear that matters were reaching a crisis. The Spanish Military League, an organisation of fascist army officers, had proceeded very far in the preparations for a coup. The government even discovered that weapons were being smuggled into Navarra; that Civil Guard uniforms were manufactured by unauthorised people; that suspicious officers were being moved into strategic positions.

Meanwhile strikes involving 250,000 workers continued. The Socialists and Communists, sensing the grave danger of the strikes (which embarrassed the Azaña government at a time when the fascists were using every opportunity for unrest, disorder and sabotage to provoke civil war), endeavoured to reach a settlement of the strikes at the earliest opportunity on the most favourable terms. The anarcho-syndicalists, however, not so much concerned with the problems of the People's Front, resisted. Later it was discovered that the Fascists, particularly members of the Spanish Phalanx, had received instructions to provoke extension and disorder in the strikes wherever possible. On July 6, documents were discovered on the person of arrested members of the Phalanx with instructions " to promote and foment the greatest possible number of strikes, especially in the public service."

Rumours of a monarchist revolt caused uneasiness in the city of Madrid on June 6. Reports of smuggled arms multiplied. The Communist Party appealed to the workers that the time to settle the strikes in the face of the danger of a fascist putsch had come.

On June 9 there was a revival of rumours of a fascist coup. The monarchists even spread the story that there would be an anarcho-syndicalist attempt to overthrow the government. A raid on a building led to the discovery of a number of Civil Guard uniforms.

Just one month before the fascists plunged all Spain into a welter of bloodshed, Gil Robles and Calvo Sotelo made their historical indictment, as it were, of the People's Front and laid the basis for the moral justification of their forthcoming attack. Gil Robles in the Cortes on June 17 charged that 251 churches had been burned or partially destroyed; that 269 people had been killed (160 of them Rightists, and 109, not mentioned by him, of course, slaughtered by the fascists); and that 1,500 persons had been seriously injured. He complained of the 340 strikes that had occurred since the February 1936 elections, and described the wrecking of the plants of ten Rightist newspapers.

To buttress the indictment, Calvo Sotelo made an open threat of a fascist putsch. He gave the Left Republicans in the government what actually turned out to be a last warning to break with the proletariat and peasantry. " The army," he cried, " is becoming increasingly impatient, and the government will be responsible if something happens."

Claridad, *El Socialista*, *Mundo Obrero*, *Política*, leading newspapers of the Left Parties, refuted the Robles-Sotelo charges, publishing figures of the number of workers and adherents of the People's Front assassinated, beaten, or threatened by the gangsters of the fascist armies. Addressing himself especially to the charge of desecration and destruction of churches, José Hernández, editor of *Mundo Obrero*, put the issue in this way:

" What has been responsible for the burning of the churches ? It cannot be explained simply by the hatred for the churches felt by a section of the people who have freed themselves from religious prejudices. The fact is that the churches in Spain are organisational centres of the fascists and serve as stores for their weapons. In the overwhelming majority of cases, hidden stores of arms are discovered after the churches have been set on fire. It is from these stores that people who took action against the workers' demonstrations received arms. It was in the churches that the fascists who murdered workers received sanctuary. The wrath of the masses against the churches—but not against the Catholics—which sided with reaction and fascism is understandable. There were a number of cases when it was not the people who directly set fire to the churches, but the forces of reaction which provoked the fire so as to give rise to discontent among the believers. The Communist Party explained to the masses that the burning of churches and monasteries only plays into the hands of counter-revolution."

On July 12 hell broke loose. Six hours after Lieutenant Castillo, a popular young member of the Assault Guards, a member of the Socialist Youth League, as well as of the Union of Militant Anti-Fascists, was assassinated, Calvo Sotelo was murdered. It was known in Madrid that Calvo

Sotelo had given the order for the assassination of Castillo.

The man who killed Calvo Sotelo, Spain's leading monarchist and most violent fascist, was a captain of the Civil Guard. This captain, on July 29, 1936, gave his own life at Alto de León pass in the Guadarrama Mountains in defence of Madrid. At Calvo Sotelo's funeral the fascists attempted to riot, and two of their followers were killed by the police. *Epoca* and *Ya*, Rightist newspapers, were suspended because of their provocative attack on the government in articles describing Calvo Sotelo's death.

Spain had arrived at the gravest period in its history. Socialists, Communists, Syndicalists, Left Republicans, and other upholders of the Republic knew the hour of danger had struck; but they did not fully grasp the magnitude of the danger. On July 13, three days before the Civil War began, the Socialist and Communist parties, the united youth organisations, and the U.G.T. met and pledged their staunchest unity, adherence to the People's Front, and support of the government against any fascist threat to establish a dictatorship.

" Gathered together in the quarters of the Executive Commission of the Socialist Party," read this pledge, " the representatives of the workers' forces within the People's Front have drawn up the following note:

" The proposals of the reactionary elements, enemies of the Republic and the proletariat, being known, the political and trade-union organisations represented by the undersigned have met and established absolute and unanimous agreement to offer to the government the assistance and support of the masses which follow them, for everything which signifies the defence of the regime and resistance against attacks which may be made on it.

" This agreement is not merely temporary, but on the contrary is proposed to be permanent as long as the circumstances make it advisable in order to strengthen the People's Front and fulfil the designs of the working class, placed in danger by enemies of the Republic.

" For the U.G.T., Manuel Lois; for the Federation of Socialist Youth, Santiago Carillo; for the Communist Party, José Diaz; for the House of the People, Edmundo Dominquez; for the Socialist Party, Jiminez Asuá."

After the burial of Castillo and Calvo Sotelo there was a frightening quiet in Madrid. It was the calm before the storm.

CHAPTER XI

BEHIND THE CIVIL WAR

IF IT IS TRUE that all the Spanish people were not caught wholly by surprise when the fascist revolt broke out on July 17, 1936, it is equally true that the extent, depth, and seriousness of the uprising were not fully gauged. The initial impression in official circles was that this uprising was a 1936 version of Sanjurjo's 1932 drive to Seville. The government issued statements that all was over with the rebels even as the rebellion was gathering momentum. Under other circumstances this optimism might have proved fatal.

The murder of Calvo Sotelo was more than merely an act of revenge or individual terrorism. It was a weather-vane of the fury and rage which Sotelo's repeated threats in the Cortes had awakened in great masses of people. Calvo Sotelo in his own person symbolised the parasitic interests of the monarchy, the clergy, and the landowners. He was the spokesman for these interests. His assassination was a political warning, delivered in spontaneous but unmistakable fashion, that the fifth year of the Second Republic had to be decidedly different from the first.

Calvo Sotelo's murder precipitated a government crisis in which the reactionaries had already exhausted every means of fighting back except one —rebellion. They had already walked out of the Cortes, promising never to return. They had already staged a dress rehearsal at Alcalá de Henares. They had already made their threats. The murder of Calvo Sotelo suddenly raised the ante and they could call the turn only by an actual uprising.

The rebellion was just as serious as its preparations, and these were not the work of a few hours. The original plan for the uprising called for a sudden intensive drive in practically every important centre of the country. Such a plan could not be carried out without co-ordinated action. Co-ordination on many fronts is proof of long negotiations and careful plotting.

The uprising took place almost as planned, but the gap short of perfection was of the utmost importance because it gave a wavering government time and opportunity to act with sufficient decision to weather the first shock. As subsequent events proved, the success of the uprising depended upon the perfect timing of sudden thrusts in half a dozen parts of the country, hundreds of miles apart. Generals, long accustomed to playing solos at revolt, had to co-ordinate activity to a degree which strained the probabilities of success.

The political and social aspect of the revolt had been worked out for months previously as huge sums of money mysteriously began to leave the country after the February elections, as the crops were systematically sabotaged for the sake of an enforced hunger in the villages and cities, as the reactionary deputies rose in the Cortes to inflame their followers against the Republic. But between the social and political side and the military side there was a decided division of labour. When the uprising broke out, the generals took command.

The military uprising rested upon eight key generals. These men constituted virtually the entire general staff under Gil Robles in 1935. They were Generals Francisco Franco, Manuel Goded, Queipo de Llano, Emilio Mola, Joaquin Fanjul, Miguel Cabanellas, Domingo Batet, and José Sanjurjo. They were double the number of horsemen who had led a previous apocalypse.

Of the eight, Sanjurjo was undoubtedly the oldest, best known, and most adept insurgent. Every time the Communists warned of imminent rebellion, they recalled the escapade of Sanjurjo in 1932. He was sixty-four years old by this time, with a long and successful career behind him. He had been an intimate of Primo de Rivera's and a faithful supporter of the dictatorship, the " Lion of the Riff." In 1923 he served as military governor of Saragossa. At the time of the 1931 revolution he held the key position of commander of the Civil Guards. After the establishment of the Republic he was demoted to the command of the Cara- bineros—practically an insult.

After his unsuccessful revolt of August 1932 was put down, he stood trial for his life in a Madrid military tribunal. His attorney defended him mainly by attacking the Socialists, a strategy cal- culated to appeal to the President, Alcalá-Zamora, in whose power it lay to commute a death-sentence to life imprisonment.

" General Sanjurjo tried to save Spain from Socialism, a thing others deemed necessary," his attorney thundered.

The General was sentenced to death, but his sentence was commuted as expected. He was even- tually set free after serving a short prison sentence in Cádiz. After that he went into forced exile in Portugal. A general had not died in Spain for treason since 1841.

The career of Franco was possibly more lustrous, but very similar. He was considered something of a prodigy, only forty-five years old and the youngest general in the army. Franco was first appointed to the post at the age of thirty-two. He earned a reputation as commander of the Foreign

Legion in Morocco, where he served from 1921 until 1926. In the campaign against the Asturian workers in 1934, he became associated with that short but descriptive title " The Butcher." It was frequently said in the 1935 period that as Gil Robles's chief of staff he was being groomed to play Göring to the Hitler of either Gil Robles or Calvo Sotelo. When the political tide swung over again to the left after the election of February 1936, Franco was cleaned out of the War Ministry and sent packing into " exile " to the Canary Islands, where it was thought he would be safe from mischief. This was another case where a reactionary's wings were scared but not clipped by the republicans.

Before Franco filched the title, Emilio Mola was generally considered the best-hated man in Spain. He, too, received his apprenticeship in the Alfonso and Primo de Rivera periods. In the two Cabinets which intervened between Primo de Rivera and the Republic he served as National Director of Police, a job which put him in a position to deal ruthlessly with strikes, radical meetings, and peasant unrest. A month before the Republic was ushered in, Mola suddenly resigned and disappeared. When the Socialist-Republican coalition took office, he was one of the first men they sought. He was wanted on a charge of murder of workers in November 1930, when police fired into a funeral procession at his orders. Mola suddenly turned up, and the trial was held, but generals were immune. Franco brought him back to active service.

General Queipo de Llano is another of the monarchy's bequests to the Republic. He made some revolting blunders in the campaign against the Riffs and was summarily removed from action in Morocco by the Primo de Rivera government in 1924. Queipo de Llano did very badly under the monarchy after that. In December 1930 he collaborated with Ramón Franco (brother of Francisco, and latterly the Spanish air attaché in the Washington, D.C., Embassy), in a vaguely anti-monarchist revolt at Cuatro Vientos, the Madrid military airport. The revolt was short-lived and both Franco and Queipo de Llano made for Portugal, a friendly haven for embarrassed Spanish generals. When Francisco Franco took office, he was brought back and put in charge of the Seville garrison.

General Domingo Batet is the man who broke the Catalan revolt in 1934 and sent Luis Companys to a thirty-year jail sentence. Companys made the mistake of sending him an advance notice of the revolt and giving him an hour to choose sides. Batet, in command of the Barcelona garrison, had his men in the streets in half an hour and Companys in jail soon after.

The rest of the eight all had similar if less

notorious careers. They were run-of-the-mill
Spanish generals who had learned what they knew
under the monarchy and tolerated the Republic
only as long as they lacked the power to overthrow
it.

The plan of revolt called for Franco to come up
from the Canary Islands to take command of
Morocco. Goded, exiled by the Republic to the
Balearic Islands, was to fly to Barcelona and take
charge with Batet. Queipo de Llano was already
in position in Seville, Mola at Burgos in the north,
Cabanellas at Saragossa in the north-east. Sanjurjo
was to come in from Lisbon.

From Seville, Franco and Queipo de Llano were
to drive forward to the west in the Badajoz region,
while Mola's forces came down from the north.
The southern and northern wings of the fascist
army were then to unite for a joint assault against
Madrid.

The uprising broke out on July 17 in Ceuta and
Melilla, in Spanish Morocco, and in Las Palmas,
Canary Islands. Franco was already in position.
Madrid and Barcelona were still quiet at this time
and the government prematurely announced that
Morocco had been pacified. Meanwhile, despite
the official optimism, Queipo de Llano occupied
Seville, and Mola and Cabanellas began operations
in the north.

In Madrid and Barcelona the revolt served to

give the government the jitters, but it was quelled in both places by the afternoon of July 20.

The greatest weakness of the rebels was in Madrid. The Left Republican government, right after the 1936 election, had sent all of the most notorious insurgents out of the capital, and this left a big gap in the plans. Fanjul, who had no command, was entrusted with the work of rallying the Madrid garrisons.

In Madrid the insurgents never succeeded in coming into the streets, although the plot had been meticulously prepared. The only serious fighting occurred in the shelling of the Montana barracks under the command of General Fanjul. A correspondent of the London *Times* later gave the following vivid account of the Madrid episode:

"At dawn, Monday, July 20, the uneasy slumbers of the city were startled by heavy explosions. From roof-tops smoke and firing could be seen out at the aerodrome of Cuatro Vientos and in the cantonments of Carabanchel, Getafe, and Vicalcaro; but the only heavy firing was in town, the Montana barracks raised the white flag after four hours' bombardment, for the rank and file did not desire to fight against the constituted authority of the Republic.

"Many fascists and officers perished at the embrasures and parapets. Resistance weakened and the men rebelled and drove most of the

Ks

remaining officers into the central courtyard. There the onrushing forces found them with cadets and Black Shirts. A machine gun dispatched many. The dead in the barracks were estimated at 200, but no authentic figure is known.

" Out in the cantonments several officers were shot when they tried to influence their regiments in classic style by bombastic pronunciamentos. Militia, police, and aircraft cowed the rest.

" Through lack of initiative from the Montana barracks, inadequate seconding by the military camp and other barracks in Madrid, and, above all, through the uncertainty of the support of the men in the ranks, a movement otherwise meticulously prepared was killed. The artillery was all in the hands of the insurgents. Bolts of spare rifles had been conveyed secretly to the Montana barracks. All the government could muster was one heavy gun and two field pieces, collected from the repair shops, with 5,000 old rifles.

" The guns were drawn by trucks from a beer factory, and a crew was improvised. This hastily formed battery carried an element of surprise and was more than a match for the trench mortars of the Montana barracks."

There was more fighting in Madrid after the surrender of La Montana, but most of it was between snipers and desperadoes and workers' militiamen.

In Barcelona the rebels were more fortunate because their strategy was better timed. In the dead of night on Sunday, July 19, 5,000 regular troops, under fascist command, marched into the heart of the city and occupied strategic positions in the Hotel Colón and the Plaza de Cataluña. They were strongly entrenched in the middle-class districts as well as near the water-front working-class section, where they occupied the Customs House, artillery barracks, and the Columbus Monument.

When daylight broke, the situation was immediately critical, but news of the coup soon spread throughout the city. Barricades, thrown up by the workers with heavy cobblestones torn out of the pavement, made their appearance by ten o'clock in the morning. Few workers were armed, however, and had the fascists attacked in the very early hours of the morning, it is probable that success would have been theirs. In the afternoon the government executed an excellent stroke by broadcasting an order for the complete demobilisation of the army. The rank and file of the insurgents became restless, and four hundred troops immediately changed sides at Barcelona University.

Most important of all, Companys did not repeat the fatal error of 1934 and he threw the arsenals open to the people. After fierce and bloody street fighting, the fascist command, including General Goded, was captured by 4 p.m.

Within a week many thousands of workers, estimated at about fifty thousand, had been armed and organised into Workers' Militia units. In co-operation with the Civil Guards and the police, they took charge of Barcelona and Madrid, patrolling the streets, fighting snipers, and organising the food supply. As the seriousness of the revolt was appreciated and the danger to Madrid from Mola's men beyond the Guadarrama Mountains became known, more and more workers, men and women, were recruited for front-line action.

The Anti-Fascist Militia Committee of Catalonia was set up after brief negotiations on July 22. The various left groups in the Committee agreed upon a statement of aims. This document, the first joint effort successfully carried through by all the antifascist forces in Spain, stated:

COMMITTEE OF ANTI-FASCIST MILITIA OF CATALONIA

PROCLAMATION

In accordance with the decree published by the Catalan Generalidad in the Official Bulletin of to-day, the constituted committee of the Anti-Fascist Militia of Catalonia has made the following decisions which are binding on all citizens:

1. Revolutionary order is hereby established, the maintenance of which all organisations belonging to the Committee are responsible.

2. The Committee has appointed the necessary agencies charged with strictly enforcing the ordinances of the Committee in order to maintain control and vigilance. Towards this end, these agencies shall carry corresponding credentials for the purpose of identification.

3. These agencies will be the only ones duly accredited by the Committee. All who act independently of them will be considered opponents and will have to suffer the consequences of the punishment determined by the Committee.

4. Night officers will be especially strict against all who attempt to interfere with revolutionary order.

5. From 1 to 5 a.m. the streets will be open to the following: (a) those duly accredited by the organisations which constitute the Militia Committee; (b) Persons accompanied by one of the foregoing, and whose trustworthiness is vouched for; (c) those who, by force of circumstances, are compelled justifiably to leave their homes.

6. For the purpose of recruiting members into the Anti-Fascist Militia, the organisations that constitute the Committee are authorised to open recruiting stations and training grounds.

Conditions for such recruiting will be formulated in detail through private communication.

7. The Committee expects, in view of the necessity of establishing revolutionary order against the fascist bands, that it will not have to resort to disciplinary measures to enforce its decisions.

Barcelona, July 22, 1936.[1]

The rebels were in strong positions owing to the very momentum and shock of their initiative. Spain is divided into eight military divisions, with headquarters at La Coruña, Burgos, Valladolid, Saragossa, Madrid, Seville, Valencia, and Barcelona. Of these the rebels held all but Madrid and Barcelona. They were occupying Burgos, Valladolid, Salamanca, Gijón, Oviedo, and Pamplona in the north-west, Saragossa and Huesca in the north-east, Toledo in the centre, and Seville, Cádiz, Cáceres, and Córdoba in the south, as well as all of Spanish Morocco and the Balearic Islands. They, too, were the victims of optimism, however. On Wednesday, July 22, *La Unión*, the fascist paper in Seville, announced in banner headlines on page one that " the Valladolid

[1] The Committee, as reported by *El Diluvio*, a Republican daily published in Barcelona, of July 22, was composed as follows: Catalan Left, Artemio Aguadé, Jaime Miravitlles, J. Pons; Catalan Action and Republican Left parties, Tomás Fábregas; Share-croppers Union, José Torrens; Marxist parties, José Miret Musté, José Rovira Canal; National Confederation of Labour, José Acea, Buenaventura Durruti, Juan García Oliver; Iberian Anarchist Federation, Aurelio Fernández, D. A. de Santillán; General Workers' Union, José del Barrio, Salvador González, Antonio López.

column has entered Madrid," " Indalecio Prieto has fled by aeroplane to Portugal and ' La Pasionaria ' has been arrested at Salamanca."

The armed forces split much more evenly than the fascists had considered possible. When the uprising broke out, there were about 235,000 men under arms. Of the regular troops, 117,350 were stationed in various garrisons on the mainland, and 38,000 regulars, Foreign Legionnaires, and Moors were in Morocco. In addition, there were 32,000 Civil Guards, 16,000 Carabineros, 17,000 Assault Guards, and 18,000 sailors. The fascists had counted upon ninety per cent of these men.

In actual fact, only the great majority of the regular troops—about seventy-five per cent—came over to the rebels, thanks mainly to Franco's selective recruiting during his regime in the War Ministry. The Civil Guards were more equally divided, depending mainly upon which side controlled the region. This was singularly unfortunate for the fascists because the Civil Guards fought on the side of the government in Madrid and Barcelona. About the same large percentage of Assault Guards supported the government as did regular troops the rebels.

The rebel forces, however, constituted the only trained forces in the country. The Moroccan troops were the only hardened and experienced fighters. In the north the rebel forces were largely recruited from volunteers, as were the government defenders, but this was not at all true in the south, where the transport of troops from Morocco was possible. By the middle of August some of the Moroccan troops were successfully moved into the north after the capture of Badajoz.

But in two of the country's defence divisions the fascists suffered distinct setbacks. They had never made great headway among the air force, and the republicans had always counted upon holding the aviators in line. This was due to the fact that the very recent establishment of the air force had prevented the same remnants of feudalism from taking root as in the army. Technical requirements forced recruiting from the middle class instead of " gentlemen's sons."

In the navy, too, the republicans were dominant. Again, social derivation was decisive. The strenuous life of the seamen had little in common with parasitism. Conditions aboard ship in practically every navy are notoriously harsh, and left-wing propaganda in the navy was also very powerful.

The loyalty of a large part of the navy decisively prevented Franco from transporting large numbers of Moroccan troops to the mainland in the first two weeks of the war. The naval patrol in the south made transport by sea extremely hazardous. Franco was forced to resort to aeroplane passage, but this was slow work. In this respect, again, the government was given a chance to organise defence and take stock.

But the chief and perhaps fatal weakness of the fascists was their lack of a mass basis among the people, except in Old Castile and Navarra, in the north beyond the Guadarramas. As soon as the government began to arm the workers, it was able to draw upon inexhaustible military and human resources. Men and women, many of whom had never handled a gun, gladly sped to the front. A fascist victory under these conditions could only be a victory of total extermination. The people surrendered their arms only to death.

In the south the fascists were operating in extremely hostile territory. Before Queipo de Llano gained control of Seville, for example, he was forced to shell and demolish the workers' quarters of the city. Long years of warfare had taught the Spanish people the art of guerrilla warfare. Even when the rebels gained their objective, it was at a terrible cost and they found it impossible to squeeze all the fruits of victory for want of adequate policing. Danger to their rear prevented them from plunging ahead too rapidly. This was especially evident in the rebel drive from Seville to Badajoz. Badajoz, on the Portuguese border, was finally taken, but it was a region where the peasants were most radicalised, where they had divided the land without official ceremony.

Superficial calculation in the first days of the war gave the rebels half the country. The rebel half extended from Saragossa in the north-east all the way to the Atlantic, with the exception of a narrow slice in the extreme north near Bilbao, then in a great arc from Saragossa to Córdoba, Granada, and Seville. The government controlled the whole eastern half of the country, including all the big seaports, except Cádiz. Such calculations, however, were hardly valid, because many fascist positions were islands in hostile territory and the rebels could not afford to send punitive expeditions into the countryside.

Another important factor in the struggle was the circumstance that the government territory was far more densely populated than the rebel half. It was estimated by the newspaper *Ahora*, on August 19, that there were 15,000,000 people in the government half and 8,000,000 in the rebel half.

Considerations such as these forced General Franco to resort to Moorish troops in the struggle against the Spanish people. For centuries the Moors had been hunted and hounded out of Spain and then reconquered in Morocco. Sanjurjo had gained the title " Lion of the Riff " in just such a campaign back in the 'twenties. Franco had established himself as a cruel and efficient fighter in these campaigns. The fascist high command sought to turn the justifiable enmity of the Moors against the Spanish ruling class into anti-government channels. At the same time they knew that this was risky because it would inevitably rouse counter-sentiments even among their own supporters who had been taught to regard the Moors as fit only for slaughter. The importation of the Moors throws a curious light on the fascist claims of popular support and lends credence to the People's Front claim that fascism could be saddled on dead Spaniards only.

Apart from the fascists and the regular troops, the most important supporting strength to the rebel cause came from the Foreign Legion, stationed in Morocco, and the Carlists, who enrolled *en masse* in General Mola's northern army.

The Foreign Legion of Spain has always been most notorious for its riff-raff and common criminals. It is recruited from the human dregs of every country in the world, and even in Morocco is separated from contact with humanity. It is isolated from every human influence in a great encampment twenty miles east of Ceuta. This garrison has its own supply of food, munitions, prostitutes, and hospitals. No legionnaire leaves the encampment alone until his five-year enlist-ment period has expired. No attempt is made to raise the most primitive standards of social responsibility, because the work of the Foreign Legion is completely debasing.

Wearing red berets with green armlets on which rests a red cross, the Carlists are a colourful lot, but their cause is touched with the fantastic.

The Carlist dispute started back in 1830 when the reigning monarch, Fernando VII, changed the order of succession to the throne with the Pragmatic Sanction of April 5, 1830. Since 1713 Spain had observed the so-called Salic Law of Succession, which permitted the male line only to succeed to the throne. Fernando's brother, Don Carlos, was expected to succeed him as Carlos V.

Fernando, however, was married for the third time, in 1829, to Maria Cristina and a child, Isabel, was born to them on October 10, 1830. Maria Cristina immediately began a pressure campaign upon her husband for a change in the line of succession in favour of their daughter. Fernando finally succumbed. Don Carlos and his supporters were furious and forced Fernando to change his decision in September 1832, as the King was expected to die. But Fernando, it turned out, recovered and again changed his mind about the succession in favour of his daughter.

From this time on, the monarchists were divided into two irreconcilable factions, and the Carlist pretenders to the throne never tired of active civil war for forty years. Theirs was a lost cause and now only their hatred for the Republic remained. The fascists benefited therefrom.

On the government side fought the whole labour, republican, and nationalist movement.

The Communists, Socialists, and anarchists for the first time in Spanish history fought side by side. In 1933 their division had proved fatal. In 1936 even the anarchist leaders declared in favour of the republican government in the early days of the fighting. An epoch in modern Spanish labour history was marked when the leaders of the syndicalist National Confederation of Labour issued an appeal to the workers of Saragossa, in rebel hands, to support the government. This was a marked departure from their old policy of lumping fascists, republicans, Socialists, and Communists together in one bag and beating them with the same stick of doctrine.

What characterised the position of every tendency in the labour movement was that all immediately put differences aside in favour of the all-important immediate task before them, that of defending the Republic against the fascist onslaught.

In the early part of August the French Communist paper *L'Humanité* published the following statement:

" The Central Committee of the Communist Party of Spain requests us to inform the public, in reply to the fantastic and tendentious reports published by certain newspapers, that the Spanish people, in their struggle against rebellion, are not striving for the establishment of the dictatorship of the proletariat, but know only one aim: the defence of the republican order, while respecting property.

" This work for the welfare of the country has the co-operation of all social strata of the working population and of all organisations, not only of the Republican, Communist, Socialist, Syndicalist parties, but of such conservative parties as the Basque Nationalist Party, whose members are Catholics. This fact gives the lie to the declarations made by General Franco on the ' Marxist danger ' in Spain, and demonstrates the duty imposed on all order-loving persons, without exception, to take sides with the defenders of order in Spain."

Largo Caballero, the foremost leader of the Spanish Socialists, made a very similar declaration to a correspondent of the Paris *Soir* on July 24:

" Until now there were three trends in the Spanish labour movement. During these last few months many elements of dissension were removed, but there still remained many things which divided us. As soon as we received the first warning that the generals, combined with all the forces of reaction, were preparing the decisive struggle, the United Front was set up one hundred per cent.

"I have just come from Madrid, where until now there were divergent opinions between moderate Socialists, radical Socialists, Communists, Syndicalists, and Anarcho-Syndicalists. In a single day all these divergencies disappeared, and we immediately formed committees composed of the representatives of all trends. There are no more differences of party among Spanish republicans. There exists only the great mass of those who are ready to sacrifice their lives to free Spain from the nightmare of ever-threatening reaction. We must make an end of all these seditious elements, the grandees, the generals."

In the same vein the Iberian Anarchist Federation (F.A.I.) and the syndicalist National Confederation of Labour (C.N.T.) issued an Information Bulletin during the fighting in which they stated their position. The English edition of the bulletin gave " the present position of the F.A.I. and the C.N.T." as follows:

" F.A.I.'s attitude on the [anti-fascist] Committee [in Barcelona] has been of great moderation. The C.N.T. is using every effort to bring back normal life. It has called off the general strike and enforced the immediate settlement of all pending disputes. Certain enterprises deserted by their

owners have been taken over by the workers under
the direction of their syndicates (trade unions),
but there is no immediate intention of introducing
Anarchist Libertarian Communism.

" The really important thing which takes
precedence over everything else is the great
struggle against fascist militarism."

The government changed premiers three times
in the first three days of the fighting. On July 18,
as reports of revolts throughout the country started
coming into the capitol, Premier Santiago Casares
Quiroga, leader of the Galician Federation,
resigned. President Manuel Azaña commissioned
the speaker of the Cortes, Diego Martínez Barrios,
head of the Republican Union Party, to form a
Cabinet. Martínez Barrios formed a Cabinet
slightly to the right of the previous one and it lasted
only eight hours. The Minister of Marine, José
Giral Pereira, then came to the helm and formed a
new Cabinet, practically identical to that of
Martínez Barrios with two exceptions. Giral
Pereira was a member of President Azaña's Left
Republican Party.[1]

Giral Pereira issued this statement late in August

[1] The Giral Cabinet was composed as follows : Premier and Minister of
Marine, José Giral Pereira ; War, General Luis Castello ; Foreign Affairs,
Agusto Barcia ; Agriculture, Mariano Ruiz Funes ; Public Works, Antonio
Velayo ; Communications, Bernardo Giner de los Ríos ; Industry and
Commerce, Placido Alvarez Buylla ; Interior, General Pozas ; Treasury,
Enrique Ramos ; Justice, Manuel Blanco Garzon ; Labour, Lluhi
Esquerra ; Public Instruction, Francisco Barnés.

in which he clearly identified the two sides in the war:

" The present situation in Spain has been provoked by the military, the clergy, and the fascists in an open rebellion against the Republic and the legitimate government elected by the people.

" The existing Madrid government is republican, without one Socialist or Communist minister, but with the support of these parties. Campaigning against reaction and fascism and to obtain the fruition of its programme, the People's Front agreed to a popular general election last February.

" This damaged the privileges of the ultra-conservatives, who are now rebelling."

While the government supporters all insisted that the war was one between the Republic and fascism, the rebels insisted that their fight was against Communism. General Franco himself had a lively appreciation of the international as well as the national importance of the fascist uprising. He issued a statement on July 21 in which he charged that two Soviet tankers, armed with two guns, had bombarded Ceuta. He continued: " The interests of Spain therefore are not alone at stake as our trumpet call sounds across the Strait of Gibraltar." On another occasion he declared that the aim of the rebellion was " to save Spain and western Europe from the menace of Russian Communism."

Ls

A most interesting and revealing interview was given to the Paris *Soir* by Gil Robles on July 30 before his departure for Portugal. As usual, Gil Robles began slightly to the left and ended far to the right. The whole interview follows:

CORRESPONDENT: " It is said that you have taken an active part in the rebellion."

GIL ROBLES: " That is false. I decline all material and moral responsibility. After the last election, which resulted in a victory of the Left, I constantly repeated in every Cortes and in public meetings that I would fight the government by parliamentary means only. But I also told the Prime Minister and the Minister of the Interior—and several times too—that they had to stop the development of the extremely dangerous situation. They should have put an end to the strikes and to the attacks while there was yet time. I always foresaw what was coming."

CORRESPONDENT: " What do you think of the generals who are leading the rebels ? "

GIL ROBLES: " I know them all very well. It is evident that—as Minister of War—I was in constant contact with them. They are certainly all patriots. They wished to force the government to take energetic measures against the terror of the extremists or to oblige the government to leave the hands of the army free to re-establish order and sweep out anarchy. The government answered the ultimatums of Franco and Sanjurjo with the order to fire. Another solution would have been preferable: to have given the Ministry of War to General Franco. Extraordinary times require extraordinary measures. Even after the debarkation of the first Moroccan troops at Algeciras, there was still time to avoid a civil war if the government was willing to compromise."

CORRESPONDENT: " But the generals have formed a provisional government."

GIL ROBLES: " That is correct. But they have done so only on the sixth day of the revolt after it was clear that they could not negotiate and that only two solutions remained: either a Spain governed by a military dictatorship or a Communist Spain."

CORRESPONDENT: " Then you support a military dictatorship ? "

GIL ROBLES: " In the present situation it seems to me that a military dictatorship could be considered a transitional government. But Franco, Mola, and Queipo de Llano, after having driven the government from Madrid and freed Barcelona, will have to form a government including civil technicians. Only on this condition will reorganisation be effective. What our country needs above all is peace, in order to be able further to organise all the Rightist parties, starting with the Carlists and finishing with the fascist formations of de Rivera, in a vast movement of reconstruction."

An interview between General Franco and Jay Allen of the *Chicago Daily Tribune*, published on July 27, showed that Gil Robles and Franco were giving pretty much identical answers. Among other things, Allen asked:

" What of labour unions ? "

" They are all right when not poisoning the workers with the doctrine of class warfare," was the reply.

Later on, Allen asked: " Would your government be a military or a civilian dictatorship ? "

" A military dictatorship, and later on we would have a plebiscite for the nation to decide what it wanted," said Franco.

And on programme:

ALLEN : " What is your programme ? "

FRANCO : " All possible reforms within the capacity of the nation's economy. We balk at nothing that the country's economy can stand."

ALLEN : " Agrarian reform ? "

FRANCO : " No use in giving poor land to poor peasants. It is not land alone that counts, but money to work it. Another twenty-five years will see the natural break-up of the big estates into small properties and the creation of a bourgeois peasantry."

When it is recalled that the Nazi programme in

Germany before 1933 included many highly provocative and radical-sounding planks about division of the land, confiscation of wealth, and the like, it would appear that the Spanish fascists were not even promising very much in advance.

As the war progressed, atrocity legends multiplied. Atrocity stories are the easiest to make and the hardest to prove. Atrocities, moreover, breed atrocities. Rarely has any civil war produced a bigger crop of them, owing, perhaps, to modern innovations for their transmission. At any rate, it must be remembered that the burning of churches in one country may be the most common and traditional channel of popular resentment while in others it may amount to the most horrible kind of desecration.

A revealing cable was sent by Robert Neville, correspondent of the *New York Herald-Tribune*, dated Tangier, Morocco, August 21:

" In Gibraltar, I found to my surprise that most of the newspapermen had been sending only ' horror ' stories. They do not seem to be awake to the terrible international implications in this situation.

" One widely known war correspondent arrived with two blonde secretaries, sixteen trunks, and a couple of radio receiving sets. The correspondents have specialised in Red Terror whereas the writer of this dispatch has been the witness of White terror in Granada for twenty-three days."

Although the international Press, or a large section of it, was full of " horror " stories, with special emphasis on the " Red terror " angle, the bloodiest slaughters on the rebel side seem to have been committed after the capture of Badajoz and Irun by Moroccan troops. Foreign Legionnaires, accustomed to long years of ruthless slaughter in the colonies, simply continued their ordinary tactics on the mainland. When General Franco broadcast the warning that not a " Marxist " would be left alive if he seized the capital, his threat did not make life safer for his supporters who had the misfortune to be in Madrid at the time. At any rate, a telegram from the British colony in Madrid to Foreign Minister Anthony Eden in London stated, as quoted in the *New York Times*, August 15, that " the British colony of Madrid indignantly repudiates the hysterical stories published in the British Press by refugees from here which are causing unnecessary anxiety to relatives."

CHAPTER XII

A WORLD WAR LOOMS

FROM THE VERY START, Spain's Civil War was given a broader framework by the more ominous danger of a world war. Indeed, the fascist coup and its subsequent devastating fighting was always overshadowed by the perspective of its sinking into the relative unimportance of a Sarajevo before the war of 1914.

Of all the spots on the globe previously chosen for the origin of the next world war, Spain was the last place considered by political commentators. But so fraught with danger of war is the world, primarily because of the fascist desire for colonial conquest and territorial redivision, that any pretext may serve for beginning the holocaust that is generally believed inevitable.

Adolf Hitler and Benito Mussolini had previously left the world without the slightest doubt that their chief aim in the furtherance of their fascist regimes was territorial expansion. Mussolini was in the very final act of subjugating the last of " free " Africa, Ethiopia. Hitler was negotiating with Great Britain for the return of the former German colonies in Africa or preparing for war to make the Soviet Ukraine German territory. " Say it with colonies," was Hitler's favourite slogan. Thus, when General Francisco Franco began the Civil War against the Spanish government by seizure of Spanish Morocco, and his associates took command in the Balearic Islands, both Italy and Germany saw their opportunity of making colonial gains in the decisive areas of the western Mediterranean. We have already pointed out that Mussolini had established cordial relations with Dictator Primo de Rivera of Spain in 1925. At that time they acted jointly against France and Great Britain. Mussolini was then too engrossed in strengthening Fascism at home to make the maximum use of this collaboration. But when the Spanish Civil War began in 1936, he had won his first victory against Great Britain in East Africa and the Mediterranean approaches to Suez.

The prize offered by General Franco for adequate fascist aid was enough to make both Hitler and Mussolini risk a world war. Ceuta, dangled before Mussolini, is a fortified city in Spanish Morocco almost directly opposite Gibraltar. In Italian hands, strongly and modernly fortified, it could immediately destroy British control of the European entrance to the Mediterranean. The Balearic Islands, just beyond Gibraltar, are admirably situated to cut the Gibraltar–Malta route of the British. For Mussolini the Spanish colonial prizes were most desirable. The Italian Mediterranean chain would then comprise Palermo (Sicily), Cagliari (Sardinia), Port Mahon (Minorca, Balearic Islands), and Ceuta (Morocco). Each of these stepping-stones in the Mediterranean is within a half-day's sailing distance of the next.

Add to these the strongly fortified position along the west coast of the Red Sea, where Italy rules in Eritrea, Ethiopia, and Italian Somaliland, and Mussolini could feel himself infinitely closer to the new Roman Empire than the costly Ethiopian war had left him. The route to India, under these conditions, would be threatened at Ceuta and the Strait of Bab-el-Mandeb. For Nazi Germany, the Balearic or possibly the Canary Islands would be a jumping-off place for Africa proper, either by further conquest or as a more convincing bargaining point with Great Britain.

More decisive still for Germany was the key question of placing a fascist ally in France's rear who might prove decisive in the inevitable war that Berlin sees coming. Berlin looked at a movement against France as a counter-weight to the Franco-Soviet mutual-assistance pact, an arrangement that has set up the greatest difficulties for the ambitions so crudely expressed in Hitler's autobiography *Mein Kampf*.

Evidence of the unquestionable agreement between the German, Italian, and Spanish fascists for mutual aid to defeat the legally constituted Spanish government is contained not only in the positive actions of the two fascist powers, but in reliable testimony from important sources.

" There is good reason to believe," declared the *Manchester Guardian* on August 5, 1936, " that the German government knew of the plans for the rebellion long before it began. The Spanish General Sanjurjo was in Berlin, where he conducted secret negotiations regarding Spain." The London *Daily Herald* of August 1, 1936 reported that German bombing planes, which were loaded at Hamburg for the Spanish fascists in July, had been ordered by General Sanjurjo in March.

On July 25, 1936 the *Manchester Guardian* revealed that Italian and German fascist support to the Spanish reactionary insurgents was pledged for a consideration. " During the last week," said the *Guardian*, " large numbers of Italian and German agents have arrived in Morocco and the Balearic Islands. These agents are taking part in military activities and are also exercising a certain political influence. For the insurgents the belief that they have the support of two great powers is an immense encouragement, for many of the weapons now in their hands are of Italian origin. This is primarily so in Morocco." To this the *Guardian* added: " The

German influence is strongest in the Balearic Islands. Apparently she hopes to secure concessions there."

London's belief in a previous Italian, German, and Spanish fascist understanding was summed up by the Hearst Press correspondent William Hillman, on August 12, 1936. This correspondent, employed by the most friendly agent of the fascists in the United States, outlined the details of the fascist agreement concerning Spain as follows:

" 1—If Franco succeeds in establishing a stable *de jure* government, Italy would provide a loan to revive industry in Spain and help the nation through a period of reconstruction.

" 2—Such a loan would be guaranteed by a lien on the Spanish railroads.

" 3—A ' defensive pact ' would be concluded between the two governments.

" 4—Unless obstacles arising prevent it, Franco would cede to Italy the strategic port of Ceuta in Spanish Morocco and the Island of Minorca in the Mediterranean. If actual sovereignty cannot be transferred because of diplomatic impediments, Franco would give Italy the right to establish naval bases at these important places."

With such currency, the Spanish fascists could buy all the arms necessary from the two accomplice fascist powers.

On August 14, 1936 the Madrid government declared it had seized documents proving implication of the German government in the Spanish fascist plot, payment for which was to be not only the alliance of a fascist Spain against a People's Front France, but also substantial concessions in Spanish Morocco and the Balearic Islands.

The *Manchester Guardian* added that: " On the Spanish mainland Germany controls a large and extremely well-organised branch of the National Socialist Party. This branch has been strongly reinforced during the past few weeks (that is, before the outbreak of the Fascist coup) by newcomers from Germany. She also controls a powerful organisation for political and military espionage which works behind a diplomatic and educational façade."

On August 18 the London *News Chronicle* published documents revealing the existence in Spain of a vast network of Nazi espionage and terrorist organisations. Spies made periodic reports on all Germans in Spain from the humblest émigré to the Ambassador. Secret tribunals were set up all over the country to punish those who offended the Nazi agents. The *News Chronicle* backed up its sensational exposure with a facsimile, never denied, of one of the secret reports sent to Berlin by the chief Nazi spy in Madrid on May 2, 1934. This document was headed " Strictly Confidential ! "

and fell into the hands of the Catalonian government with a mass of other material in a raid on
the Nazi centre in Barcelona. This report went as
follows:

" Count von Welszeck, Ambassador: I hear he
has already been admitted to the Party.

" Dr. Voelkers, Counsellor of Embassy: In
Madrid since November 1933, married to a Dutch-
woman of Malay stock. Previous activity and
political disposition unknown here.

" Dr. Mey, Counsellor of Legation: Hitherto
not been prominent in a political sense. Bachelor.
Before being admitted to the Party must be ascertained whether he conforms to the Aryan para-
graph and what he did in the war.

" Dr. Korth, Secretary of the Legation: Has a
national outlook. Took part in war. Bachelor.

" Dr. Fischer, Secretary of Legation: Only here
a short time. Bachelor. Devout Catholic. May
perhaps have been connected with the Centre
[Roman Catholic] Party formerly. In agreement
with the new regime.

" R. Enze, commercial councillor: Already
joined the Party in Barcelona. Does not take any
interest in the movement."

These were the reports in the facsimile. Of the
remainder of the staff, the document says:

" E. Larsen, head of the Embassy legal staff:
Married to a South American, once champion of

democratic ideas, now 150 per cent Nazi. No fighter. Acceptance cannot be advocated.

" F. Kolbe, Consulate Secretary: Formerly zealous Marxist. Goes with Jews and other dubious elements here. There can be no question of his admission to Party.

" Kaethe Lindner, typist-secretary: National outlook. Unmarried. Nothing in way of her admission to the Party.

" Hildegard Zipplies, typist-secretary: Formerly hostile.

" C. Zwick, clerk: Already a party member. Very active.

" R. Ebert, porter: Political nonentity. Formerly a National Socialist. Owing to lack of intellectual capacity, not admissible.

" E. Stein, gardener: Takes no part in the movement.

" HEIL HITLER !

" W.2.

" Leader of the Party group in Spain
and Deputy Foreign Commissar."

According to *Die Braune Netz*,[1] the director of Nazi espionage in Spain and emissary in unofficial matters of the German Embassy at Madrid was A. W. Claus. It may be that Claus is the author

[1] *Die Braune Netz* (*The Brown Network*), Éditions du Carrefour, Paris, 1935. An English edition has been published by Knight Publications, New York.

of the above report. *Die Braune Netz* gives the names of more than thirty Nazi agents in Spain and Portugal, including a cell director in Morocco.

For all practical purposes, Spanish Morocco was an Italian protectorate by August 20, 1936. Robert Neville, *New York Herald-Tribune* correspondent at Tangier, Morocco, reported:

" So entrenched in Spanish Morocco are the Italians becoming, it is necessary to get visas for the interior from the Italian Minister here. . . . This correspondent had opportunity to see a visa for Spanish Morocco signed not by a Spanish official, but by an Italian. It seems that Franco's *de facto* representative here is the Italian Minister."

H. R. Knickerbocker, Hearst correspondent with General Mola's forces in the north of Spain, operating from Burgos, never made any secret of the fact that the major portion of the military equipment employed by the fascists was of German origin: planes, machine guns, bombs, rifles, bullets, and helmets.

Germany had the largest number of citizens employed in Spain even in May 1933, some 4,600 out of a total of 18,420 foreigners.[1] After the conservative victory of November 1933, Gil Robles encouraged the migration of Nazis to

[1] In May 1933 the classification of the total of 18,420 foreigners reported employed in Spain was as follows: Germans, 4,645; Frenchmen, 2,894; Portuguese, 2,729; British, 1,978; Swiss, 1,294; Italians, 1,199; Cubans, 251; Americans, 176; Brazilians, 70; Mexicans, 58; Filipinos, 25; Canadians, 8.

Spain, just as Primo de Rivera favoured the influx of Italian fascist propagandists during his dictatorship.

While French supporters of the anti-fascist forces in Spain moved heaven and earth to rush armaments and other aid to the Madrid government, it has not even been charged that the French People's Front intervened in any way before the outbreak of the revolt. The French assistance never reached the provocative proportions of the two fascist powers.

For example, with the pretext that German citizens were endangered by the Civil War— begun by the fascists—the Nazi government began to berate the Madrid government, accusing it in particular of murdering four German citizens. With this excuse, the German pocket battleship *Deutschland* prevented loyal Spanish warships from bombarding Ceuta at a critical point in the fighting, when General Franco was having difficulty transporting Foreign Legion and Riff troops to the Spanish mainland. German war vessels made courtesy calls upon Spanish fascist commanders in Cádiz and Seville. Frank L. Kluckhohn, the *New York Times* correspondent with General Franco's forces on the Spanish mainland, repeatedly reported the unloading of German planes from German ships. " Twenty heavy German junker bombing planes and five German pursuit planes, manned by German military pilots arrived at rebel headquarters in Seville to-day," he cabled in August. " The aeroplanes had been landed from a ship at the rebel port of Cádiz and were then flown here." About one week later when a Spanish cruiser stopped the German freighter *Kamerun* near Cádiz, fearing it was carrying a new shipment of planes and German military aviators, the Hitler government used the incident as a pretext for ordering new and more formidable operations of the German navy in Spanish waters.

That the steamer *Kamerun* had been engaged in supplying arms to the Spanish fascists was attested to by Jay Allen, of the *Chicago Tribune*. Cabling from Tangier on August 23, 1936, Mr. Allen reported:

" Twenty-three carloads of war materials brought to Portugal by the German steamer *Kamerun* for delivery to Spain were dispatched to-day in the direction of Badajoz and Salamanca. Another thirty-three carloads will be required to complete the shipment across Portugal, which virtually adopted the status of a belligerent in Spain's five-weeks-old Civil War when she allowed the *Kamerun* to dock after Spanish loyalist warships halted and searched the vessel last week and refused to let it land at Cádiz, a rebel stronghold."

A strongly worded protest was issued, ordering

Ms

German naval commanders to fire on the next
Spanish vessel that sought to blockade a German
merchantman. A *New York Times* correspondent
cabled on September 14, 1936, during the important battle around Talavera de la Reina, that
German bombers and pursuit planes were turning the tide for the rebels. ". . . The German
aviators," he wrote, " no longer make the pretence
of wearing Spanish uniforms. . . . It can hardly be
contended that the German aviators are training
Spaniards, because these planes go off to work at
all hours of the day and there would be no need
to train aviators capable of doing bombing service. The German commander has an office
building next to General Franco's headquarters."

German planes also landed in Spanish Morocco.
Jean d'Esme, Moroccan correspondent for the
Paris newspaper *L'Intransigeant*, on July 29, 1936,
informed his paper that he had personally witnessed the arrival of a German junker plane in
Spanish Morocco. The plane had the swastika
insignia on it.

Italian assistance to the Spanish fascists was
proved much more spectacularly. During a storm
two Italian planes of a group flying to Spanish
Morocco crashed near Oran, Algeria. On August
6, 1936 General Victor Denain, High Commissioner of French Morocco, reported to his government in Paris that documents found aboard two

of the planes proved that the expedition was composed of five planes belonging to the 55th, 57th,
and 58th squadrons of the regular Italian air
force. A military pay-book found on one of the
bodies in a wrecked plane was conclusive proof
that Mussolini not only had sent his military
planes, but had ordered his officers to fight on the
side of the Spanish fascists. It was further learned
that the Italian expedition was formed at Bologna
and flew from that port on July 29 to the Elman
Aerodrome at Cagliari, Sardinia, whence it left
on July 30 for Melilla, Spanish Morocco.

The cables hummed with the news on August 18
that Mussolini had ordered the entire air fleet of
Italy to be ready for instant flight to Spain. While
this was later denied by Mussolini, he did add that
the Italian government was fully prepared to take
whatever interventionist steps it considered necessary. On the same day a party of Italian sailors
landed at Malaga and took off not only the Italian
Consul, but a number of Spanish fascists who had
taken refuge in the consulate.

Jay Allen reported in the *Chicago Tribune* of
August 5, 1936 that an Italian crew manned a
tri-motored monoplane which bombed the loyal
cruiser *Libertad* while the latter shelled the rebel
fortress of Tarifa.

" This rebel city [of Seville] has come to feel
that the presence of the Italian destroyer *Antonio*

da Noli here means that an ally has come to help the insurgents," reported Frank L. Kluckhohn in the *New York Times* of August 18, 1936. The Italian sailors were driven around Fernando Square in Spanish military trucks commandeered by the fascists.

Almost from the very day of the fascist coup the Blum government in France, in the best position to aid the Madrid government, strove to avoid international complications by appealing to the other powers for a neutrality pact. By a strict interpretation of international law, it was the right of France to render all aid requested to the legal government of Spain, which never lost its right of purchase of military supplies by the insubordination and civil war begun by the officers of the Spanish army. Whether wisely or not, however, the Blum government did make efforts to tie the hands of the German and Italian fascists diplomatically.

There then began a game of dilly-dallying, for which the Italian and especially the German fascists are notorious. This dangerous by-play was facilitated by the fact that the two hostile dictators had drawn closer to each other several months before the outbreak of the Spanish Civil War. The signing of the German-Austrian Pact, temporarily holding the Nazi "*Anschluss*" ambitions in abeyance, had drawn Berlin and Rome closer together on all European questions. The British government concurred in the French neutrality proposal of August 1, but urged the inclusion of Germany, Portugal, and Russia. The French readily accepted these additions.

By August 17, 1936, in view of the German and Italian procrastination, Augur, the famous British diplomatic commentator, could write:

" In reality it may be taken for granted that non-intervention has failed already, as supplies of war material are pouring into Spain for both the republican and militarist forces."

France set August 17 as the deadline for the neutrality pact. Though Italy answered in time to keep matters from reaching a crisis, no clear understanding was reached. Mussolini announced acceptance of the French proposals twenty-one days after they were made. He dropped previous reservations barring public subscription of funds and enlistment of volunteers on either side, although he made his adherence to the pact conditional on acceptance by Great Britain, France, Germany, Portugal, and the Soviet Union.

On August 24 the German government put an embargo on shipments of arms to Spain. Berlin's pledge of non-intervention was coupled, however, with a military move which sent a war scare through Europe. Hitler increased the term of conscription in the German army from one to two years on the pretext of the Soviet menace.

After twenty-six nations had affirmed their
" neutrality " in response to the French proposal,
a conference was held in London to inquire into
the possibility of enforcing the general agreement.
Portugal, the chief source of supplies and munitions for the rebels, did not even attend the conference. A dispatch to the *New York Times*,
September 10, described the London meeting as
follows:

" Italy and Germany again showed to-day how
easily they could obstruct the rest of Europe in the
effort to keep war supplies from Spain and prevent
the civil war from spreading.

" Consequently the first meeting of the international committee on non-intervention could not
make the slightest progress to-day, although
diplomats from twenty-six nations were present.
The two great fascist powers represented at the
committee table were not in a co-operative mood,
while little semi-fascist Portugal stayed away from
the meeting altogether."

French policy was not hard to understand. The
Blum government felt that the establishment of a
fascist State in Spain not only would increase the
danger of war but held out the certainty of France's
defeat in such a war. Therefore all of France's
interests, historical-national, anti-fascist, Socialist,
and Communist, in varying degrees imperatively

demanded effective aid to the Spanish government. But for internal reasons—fear of a Cabinet
split by the right-wing Radical Socialists—Blum
took a roundabout course.

The Blum government was severely criticised by
the revolutionary parties in France for these
manœuvres with the non-intervention pact. Both
the Socialist and Communist parties, as well as the
trade unions, continued to give the Spanish
People's Front their financial support. They took
the position that the Spanish rebels were seeking
to overthrow a democratic, constitutional government, that Italian and German intervention in
Spain threatened French security, as well as the
peace of the world, and that defeat for the Spanish
People's Front would put the Blum government in
the greatest jeopardy.

The Soviet Union felt that a free-for-all in Spain
might very well be the prologue to an even greater
war against itself. Japan would certainly not permit a period of European conflict to pass without
an attempt to seize Soviet Siberia. With war in
Europe and war in the East, the foes of the Soviet
regime could easily draw their forces together.
Soviet workers made huge contributions to the
Spanish People's Front. That world peace was
hanging in the balance in Spain was also the view
of Louis de Brouckère, the president of the Labour
and Socialist (Second) International. Early in

August, de Brouckère declared: " Peace must be
saved *now* by saving the Spanish Republic. If, for
want of courage, we permit it to be crushed, war,
pitiless war, undertaken in the most favourable
conditions, will become practically inevitable."

French aid to Spain did not all go to the People's
Front. The fascist Croix de Feu organisation gave
money, army officers, and technical specialists to
the Spanish fascists. August Heriot, a retired
French army officer, consulted with General
Franco after the latter succeeded in reaching
Seville.

British policy was confused and contradictory.
The basic concern of the British Empire is maintenance of its control of the sea route to India. In
terms of the Spanish Civil War, that interest
pointed to Gibraltar and an amenable government
in Spain proper. Tory Britain never favoured the
People's Front victories in France and Spain. But
a fascist victory could not be won without injury
to British interests. The conflicting groups within
the British Cabinet finally reached a " neutrality "
formula, with emphasis upon the determination to
safeguard Britain's vital empire links no matter
which side won. If the British Conservatives could
have procured victory for a pro-British fascist
power, they would not have hesitated to ensure
such an outcome. After a number of British planes
were received by both sides, the British Board of

Trade on August 19 finally revoked all licences for the export of arms, ammunition, and planes of either military or commercial type to Spain.

The British government also issued a stern warning against interference with her trade anywhere in Spain, meaning with the rebels. British intervention is subtle and suave, but the British have just as much at stake in Spain as Germany and Italy, or more. Before the final word has been said on the Spanish Civil War, Britain's concern will loom as a dominant factor.

Remote in the distance, the United States was also immediately involved in many issues of the war. The danger of a European war, with its Far Eastern implications, was of greatest moment. It was also marked by contradictions. On August 20, Acting Secretary of State William Phillips summarised American policy as follows: " This country is committed to the principle of non-interference in the internal affairs of other countries." For that reason, he continued, " this government will refrain from interference in the unfortunate situation which now exists in Spain. . . . The people and the government of the United States, entertaining the friendliest feeling for the Spanish people, are deeply distressed by the devastating strife that now rends that country, and earnestly hope for its termination at the earliest possible moment." On August 27, however, the State

Department associated itself with Germany and Great Britain in refusing to recognise the validity of an order by the Spanish government closing rebel ports. On September 10, however, all American warships were ordered out of Spanish waters and 500 Americans still in Spain at that time warned that they remained at their own risk.

In this complex relationship of world forces, Spanish democracy was fighting not only fascism at home but war in the world at large.

CHAPTER XIII

THE PEOPLE'S FRONT
GOVERNMENT

ONCE THE SPANISH people had taken up arms
to preserve their Republic, a new type of government of national defence became inevitable. When
the Civil War had reached a critical and decisive
stage, a People's Front Cabinet was formed for the
first time in history.

By the sixth week of the fighting, the Giral
Cabinet had not yet gone over to the offensive
which alone could have assured victory for the
Republic. On the contrary, the Civil War had
resolved itself into one of " movement " in the
south and south-east and one of " position " in the
north and north-east, in T. E. Lawrence's excellent
phrase. General Franco was driving rapidly from
the south and south-east along the Tagus River
towards Toledo and Madrid. Along the Guadarrama range, Madrid's natural barrier on the north,
the opposing forces skirmished daily, but neither
side was able to bring the battle into the other's
camp to a decisive conclusion.

The Left Republican and other middle-class
representatives in the Giral government had given
invaluable aid to the defence by their role in the
government, by their loyalty in industrial and com-
merical positions, and especially by their skill and
training in the commanding staff of the loyal
forces. Yet the brunt of the fighting and, therefore,
the fate of the Republic, unquestionably rested in
the hands of the workers and peasants. The militia
was largely composed of workers and peasants
under the leadership of the Socialist and Communist parties, the General Workers' Union, and
the syndicalist National Confederation of Labour.
Accustomed to proletarian leadership in the critical
days before the Civil War, the workers' militiamen
found the need for such guidance in the dangerous
military situation prevalent in the early part of
September especially acute.

The Giral government realised its inability to
inspire that exalted activity necessary to produce
the military miracles required to overcome the
military advantages of the fascists. This Cabinet,
it must be remembered, was mainly a coalition
between the Republican Left, headed by President
Azaña, and the Republican Union, led by the
Speaker of the Cortes, Diego Martínez Barrios.
Nevertheless, although representing only a minority either of the People's Front or of the People's
Front deputies in the Cortes, it held the confidence

of all anti-fascists: but this confidence alone was insufficient to meet military exigencies. Hence the Giral government, after fraternal discussions with the representatives of the Communist and Socialist parties, acknowledged that Spain could put forward its maximum efforts only behind a truly representative People's Front government. In such a government the proletarian parties, naturally, had to occupy a dominant position. Here was no question of the transformation of the State for socialist purposes antagonistic to the interests of the non-proletarian parties in the People's Front. In fact, a sober recognition by the middle-class parties that their interests and the further existence of the Republic would be served best by permitting the leaders of the masses to take responsibility for directing the armed people led to the formation of the People's Front government.

On September 4, when Irun, reduced to ashes, fell, the Giral government resigned, politically unblemished. Francisco Largo Caballero, Socialist idol of Spain's proletariat, assumed the premiership at the head of a People's Front government.

The new Cabinet was composed of six Socialists, two Communists, three Left Republicans, one Catalan Left, and one Republican Unionist, as follows:

Premier and War Minister: Francisco Largo Caballero, Socialist

Foreign Minister:	Julio Alvarez del Vayo, Socialist
Air and Marine:	Indalecio Prieto, Socialist
Finance:	Juan Negrin, Socialist
Commerce and Industry:	Anastasio de Gracia, Socialist
Interior:	Angel Galarza, Socialist
Agriculture:	Vicente Uribe, Communist
Education:	Jesús Hernández, Communist
Justice:	Mariano Ruiz Funes, Republican Left
Labour:	José Tomás Piera, Catalan Left
Communications:	Bernardo Giner de los Ríos, Republican Union
Public Works:	Julio Just, Republican Left
Minister without portfolio:	José Giral Pereira, Republican Left.

Largo Caballero was born on October 18, 1869. He was a plasterer by trade, and has held every important post in both the Socialist Party and the U.G.T. since 1918. He joined the U.G.T. in 1890 and came to the Socialist Party three years later. As early as 1899 he was elected to the National Executive Committee of the Socialist Party. In 1918 he was elected one of the six Socialist deputies in the Cortes, served as a Privy Councillor under Primo de Rivera, and became Minister of Labour in the Republican-Socialist government of 1931. All through this period he was the object of bitter attacks by both the anarchists and the Communists for what they considered his treacherous role in the labour movement.

Largo Caballero's career took a sharp turn after he was arrested on October 13, 1934, charged with having instigated the October uprising. He later revealed that the Socialist leaders, such as Andrés Saborit, had consciously sabotaged the plans for the uprising and had withheld instructions for the revolt until it was too late. Largo Caballero wanted to take definite action against the repressive measures of the Lerroux government after the 1933 election, but failed to win the leadership of the party over to his views. On April 3, 1934 he resigned from his position as chairman of the Socialist parliamentary group, but his resignation was refused and he was pledged to secrecy not to make the whole episode public.

On October 1, 1934 Largo Caballero, although ill, finally resigned from the post in protest against the obstructionist policy of the National Committee. Thirteen days later he was arrested for " intellectual complicity " in the October uprising and he was kept in prison without trial for thirteen months. When freed, he emerged with a new determination to swing the Socialist Party to a revolutionary course. He encouraged and supported the amalgamation of the Socialist and Communist youth movements. Although lukewarm to the People's Front policy in the beginning, he gave that movement full support when events had shown that he was mistaken.

The new Foreign Minister, Alvarez del Vayo, adhered to the Socialist left wing. He was one of Spain's best-known and most brilliant intellectuals. His fame as a journalist was exceeded only by his repute as a diplomat. He had served as Ambassador to Mexico in the first Azaña government after the establishment of the Republic.

Indalecio Prieto, a formidable figure of a man, bulging and muscular, with tremendous voice and great oratorical ability, was one of the old Socialist war-horses. Prieto was an expert at factional strife as well as a feared opponent and the recognised leader of the formerly influential " centrist " faction of the Socialist Party. The Civil War, however, had done much to heal the threatening party split. What Prieto feared most—fascist insurrection —had come to pass and parliamentary debate could no longer argue it away. Even before the formal establishment of the People's Front Cabinet, Prieto had functioned in a semi-governmental capacity in the Ministry of the Interior.

The two Communist Cabinet members, Jesús Hernández and Vicente Uribe, were the first members of their party—or of any Communist party—to participate in a Cabinet with non-proletarian party members. Hernández, the new Minister of Education, twenty-eight years of age at the time, was the youngest man ever to hold a ministerial post in the country. As editor of the Communist organ *Mundo Obrero*, and with a prestige and authority in party ranks second only to the general secretary, José Diaz, he became the chief government spokesman for the Communists. Vicente Uribe, the new Minister of Agriculture, was secretary of the Communist faction in the Cortes.

Another tradition was broken by the new Cabinet. The anarcho-syndicalists broke a seventy-year tradition by pledging their support to the new government. This anarchist reversal augured well for the ability of the new government to throw all the resources and man-power of the country against the enemy, with a minimum of friction. Anarchist support strengthened the promise that the unification of the C.N.T. and the U.G.T. might be nearer than appeared possible at the outbreak of the Civil War.

An important statement of policy was issued by the new Cabinet immediately after its first meeting :

" The government, because of its composition, considers itself the direct representative of the political forces fighting on different fronts for the maintenance of the democratic Republic against which the rebels rose in arms. The President of the Republic, Manuel Azaña, considers it necessary to

Ns

have a Cabinet with a broader base of representation. The parties to which the new ministers belong accepted the proposal at once, thus permitting the constitution of a government which included groups that, although they supported the former government, were not actually represented in it.

" The ministerial programme is based essentially on the firm intention of hastening the triumph over the rebellion by co-ordinating the people's efforts, by unity of action, to turn these efforts to best advantage. Every other political interest will be subordinated to that end. Ideological differences have been laid aside, since at present there can be no other desire than to ensure the suppression of the insurrection.

" Spain being free from all imperialistic designs, the government proclaims a policy of peace, which corresponds not only to the unanimous ideas of the ministers but to the nation's welfare, because universal peace will be the greatest guarantee for our restoration.

" In a pacific spirit the government affirms Spain's sentiments of friendship for all nations and her most devoted adherence to the Covenant of the League of Nations, in the hope that in just reciprocity our country will obtain from others the same respect it has for them.

" The government expresses its unshakable

resolve to maintain at all costs the integrity of the national territory against the danger which the success of the rebels might represent in this respect.

" The government salutes with the greatest enthusiasm the efforts of the land, sea, and air forces and the Popular Militia for defending the legality of the Republic. The government's supreme aim will be to make itself worthy of such heroic fighters, whose legitimate desire for social betterment will find in it a faithful guarantor."

This declaration served notice that the Left parties were still faithful to the policy which all of them had adopted in the first days of the war. The preservation of the democratic Republic claimed their immediate loyalty, and all differences on ultimate goal were subordinated to the defeat of fascism.

The People's Front government, like the Giral government, was primarily one devoted to the struggle against fascism and reaction, with the additional advantage that it represented and claimed the affection of broader masses. The first part of the statement of policy indicated that the change had not been forced upon the Republican Left, but, on the contrary, that President Azaña had seen the need for the new government. The presence of five middle-class representatives from all the middle-class parties in the Caballero Cabinet showed that the People's Front had

successfully weathered the transition from a
government led by the middle-class to a government guided by the workers and peasants. The
new government represented the highest stage of
the People's Front. It marked a transition from a
government supported by the People's Front to
one fully representing the People's Front.

Besides the problems of military strategy and
organisation, the defeat of fascism implied
economic steps for the speedy and effective fulfilment of the political and economic requirements
of the Republic. *Mundo Obrero* carried a significant
programmatic editorial on August 22 which set
forth the relationship between the military tasks
and the most urgent social and economic problems
from the viewpoint of the Left.

" The people, guided by their gifted political
intuition, understand that military victories must
be reinforced and consolidated with social and
political reforms. Our fight is not only to punish
the traitorous insurgents among the generals and
politicians. It is simultaneously a struggle to
reform the regime which has permitted the most
reactionary and fascist groups in society to
organise, finance, and unleash this bloody attack
upon the best sons of the people to the devastation
of Spain.

" We constantly repeat, interpreting the popular
feeling, that we are fighting for the democratic

Republic. That is certain. We are fighting, the whole people of Spain is fighting, for the democratic Republic. But neither for us nor in the spirit of the people is the word Republic an empty one. In this democratic concept we point out the deep social and economic content which the broad masses feel and understand so thoroughly. It is not even enough to take measures for economic and social transformation which, in an isolated and scattered way, the people are themselves taking.

"What is lacking now when the victorious advance of our troops recaptures surely and progressively the area of national territory in the hands of the traitors and when the final victory of the war appears as an immediate perspective, is to continue to consolidate the military victories with broad reforms of a social and economic character. This work belongs to the government. The democratic Republic means the rapid fulfilment of the division of the land, the distribution of the lands of the nobility, the great landlords, and the high clergy to the peasants and the agricultural workers, special agrarian credits, tax reduction, annulment of debts, reformation of social legislation, improvement of the conditions of life and work of the labourers. It also means measures for the protection of the small merchants and manufacturers and the legal dissolution of the reactionary and fascist parties. . . ."

The Civil War of 1936 was but a continuation, in sharper form, of the parliamentary struggle which was waged between the People's Front and the C.E.D.A. for the two preceding years. The supporters of the government took up arms in defence of their Republic and for the fulfilment of its promises. The fascists initiated a bloody civil war because their previous methods of opposition had been unsuccessful.

As always, the armed struggle was but a continuation of the political struggle by other means.

BOOK II

CHAPTER XIV

ECONOMIC ROOTS OF REVOLUTION

SPAIN has suffered for centuries not because she never attempted to leave her feudal rut but because those liberating attempts were so timid, so half-hearted, so uniformly unsuccessful. All of these political attempts to break with the feudal past foundered on economic shoals. No matter what the form of government, Spain cannot emerge into the ranks of the great nations until she has successfully mastered those basic economic and social problems which have made her, until now, such a slave to the past. In the final analysis this is the real meaning of the 1936 struggle between the Republic and its fascist enemies. The Republic signifies a degree of economic and social transformation which the fascists and all those who have rallied under their banner abhor.

It is not easy to disentangle the complicated skeins of Spanish economy. The late and uneven development of Spanish capitalism has created peculiar and contradictory problems. The majority of the people still make their living from the land, and the major portion of the wealth of the country still lies in the land. The feudal relations of production and the remains of feudal social relations are also right here—on the land with its great landowners, poor, land-hungry farmers, sharecroppers or tenants, and land labourers working for wages.

But atop the feudal basis has risen a superstructure of more modern forms of production. Although in a small minority, there are hundreds of thousands of industrial workers who must struggle not only against feudalism but against capitalism too. Spanish capitalism may be relatively undeveloped, but it is capitalism nevertheless and it contributes typical capitalist phenomena, such as strikes, unions, and revolutionary labour parties.

At the same time Spanish capitalism is capitalism with a difference. It has had a certain transforming effect upon feudalism. But feudalism has had an even greater, reciprocal effect upon capitalism. In the interaction of forces capitalism suffered because it never shook off the fundamentally contradictory forces of feudalism. In Spain alone, the forces of capitalism and feudalism never came into violent and basic collision as they did in France or in Great Britain. Capitalism and industry developed only by leave of feudal interests, so to speak. That is what accounts for the tremendous and parasitic power of the Church, the monarchy, and the grandees.

Add to all this the fact that Spanish feudalism extended into the period of imperialism which concentrated production into few hands under the dominating influence of financial barons. Modern Spain also has its imperialistic features, its colonies which it ruthlessly exploited. At the same time foreign imperialisms penetrated into Spain and with their investments obtained a stranglehold over Spanish industry.

What a complicated setting ! This is modern Spain. It is a country with feudalism existing side by side with capitalism and imperialism, on top of which are semi-colonial characteristics due to foreign financial penetration. The bottom and basic layer, however, is the feudal layer, and it is this that pulls all the rest down, throttling free industrial development, the past asphyxiating the future.

The Civil War of 1936, as well as all the political transformations of the past century, can be understood only in the light of these basic economic problems. Least understood of all the factors involved in the present situation are these forces. To evade or to misunderstand them is to make a mystery of modern Spanish history.

Until 1931 Spain was saddled with all the institutions typical of feudalism, both in its property system and in its social system. The clergy, the court, and the army were the remains of the past come to dominate the present. They were completely parasitic in their make-up. The army never won a foreign war. The Church depended mainly on ground-rent. The monarchy and the nobility were landowners and not industrial profiteers.

The dominant class in Spain, both economically and politically, was the class of great landowners, owners of typical latifundia in the old Roman sense. The basis of its wealth was great landed estates upon which toiled tenants and farm labourers not much removed from serfdom. It is estimated that out of a total population of more than 24,000,000, the large landowners added up to only about 50,000. Other estimates are far lower and place the class of grandees at 20,000 to 30,000. Numbering, at most, one five-hundredth of the total population, the grandees owned 51·1 per cent of the land. Other estimates are slightly higher. These great landowners upheld and dominated the monarchy, and all the great landowners were members of the nobility.

Slightly lower down in the scale come the wealthy farmers owning an average of 55·7 acres each. It is estimated that 700,000 of these rich farmers owned 35·2 per cent of the land. They played no independent political role and were the closest allies of the grandees of the upper strata. Of an estimated national wealth of 215,000,000,000 pesetas,[1] the landowners as a class owned 125,000,000,000.

Between the big landowners and the poor farmers, there is practically a social vacuum. The small farmers, numbering about 1,000,000, owning an average of 12·3 acres each, possess 11·1 per cent of the land. The poorest peasants, numbering about 1,250,000, owning an acre each on the average, possess 2·2 per cent of the land. They are at the bottom of the landowning pyramid.

Then there are about 2,000,000 farm labourers who work for hire. The hunger and horror of the existence of the farm labourer were inescapable. They are generally unemployed from one third to two thirds of the year. Their wages vary between 3 and 5 pesetas for a twelve- to fourteen-hour day. Out of these meagre wages the landowning employer takes a percentage for food and government taxes.

While industrial wages rose 116 per cent from 1914 to 1925, farm wages rose only 70 to 75 per cent. According to the International Labour

[1] The value of the peseta at the outbreak of the rebellion was 36·50 to the £.—Publisher of the English edition.

Office, real wages on the farm in Spain in 1930 were only 40 per cent of what they were in Great Britain at the same time. In 1931, the proportion of unemployed among the farm wage-workers was estimated at 60 per cent. That was year 1 of the Second Republic, and it was accompanied by an intense agrarian crisis.

In 1921 a Spanish financial paper published a table of the different categories of Spanish wealth. Although the differences between the various categories are no longer so great, the general relationship still holds. The table, published by the *El Financiero* on November 18, 1921, follows:

	Pesetas
Agriculture . . .	119,945,000,000
Flocks	4,000,000,000
Mines	5,000,000,000
Industry . . .	5,000,000,000
Foreign commerce . .	3,000,000,000
Coastal trade . . .	1,500,000,000
Internal trade . . .	6,000,000,000

The bourgeoisie, driving power of capitalism throughout the world, has been as weak, politically, as Spain's backward industrial and commercial development would indicate. It came into existence very late, very slowly, and very incompletely. Its weakness prevented it from playing an independent role. Needing allies in the class struggle against the proletariat, it naturally was forced to depend upon the dominant social interests, notwithstanding the fact that these interests were largely feudal and therefore essentially anti-capitalist. In a few cases, notably that of Count de Romanones, a big landowner also became an important industrialist.

Two other circumstances retarded the development of the big capitalists. Catalonia has always been the great industrial region of the country. This was historically important because Catalonia had long been treated as a colony. Secondly, the difficult development of Spanish capitalism opened the way for large-scale foreign investments, putting most of the important enterprises in foreign hands.

A more independent role has been played by the urban petty bourgeoisie, especially the artisans, small traders and shopkeepers, the lower government officials, and, above all, the intellectuals. Before 1931 they constituted the spearhead of the movement against the monarchy, the grandees, and the Church. The grandees hindered the development of industry, which would demand and assimilate middle-class technical workers. The Church monopolised the free professions, especially the teaching profession. The monarchy was a highly lucrative organisation in which the membership books had long been closed.

To-day, the most articulate, homogeneous, and decisive class in Spain are the industrial wage labourers. There are estimated to be 1,500,000

wage-workers in industry, commerce, and trans-
portation. The bulk of these are to be found in the
region of Catalonia. The chief industries in Spain
are the textile industry in Catalonia and the metal
and mining industries in the Basque country and
Andalusia. Catalonia has about 200,000 textile
workers and there are about 175,000 mine and
metal workers in the country as a whole.

Steam engines were introduced in Catalan
cotton mills as early as 1830. The first Spanish
railway was built between Barcelona and Mataro,
a distance of about thirty miles. Metallurgy
developed somewhat later around Bilbao.

The loss of colonies and then the World War
spurred Spanish industry forward. During the war
the Catalan textile industry was reorganised and
centralised. The artificial-silk industry appeared.
The chemical industry got a start. By remaining
neutral in the war, Spain was given the opportunity of filling huge orders for war materials for
both sides of the conflict. Spain had an unfavourable
balance of trade amounting to about £10,000,000
in 1913. In 1918 she had a favourable balance of
trade of about £12,000,000.

But Spanish industry is so far behind European
industry as a whole that, with the exception of a few
key industries, it resembles the status of British
capitalism in the middle of the nineteenth century.

A good index of the country's industrial development is its railroads. Rates are very high. A barrel of grapes can be shipped to London from Almería and then back to Bilbao for 5 pesetas. To send the same barrel of grapes from Almería to Madrid costs from 8 to 12 pesetas. Freight traffic in Spain in 1929 averaged two tons per inhabitant, against nine tons in France. Many towns with five to six thousand inhabitants find themselves over sixty-five miles from the nearest railway station. Spanish railroads are notorious for numerous and extended detours. The reason for these detours is that railroads were originally built more to fit the whims of the grandees than modern industrial ideas of efficiency. Everybody with influence had the railway pass near him. As a result, the distance from Madrid to Nurgos is 150 miles by highway, but 225 miles by rail.

Few of the important modern industrial enterprises are not in foreign hands. Most of the big industrial corporations are registered as Spanish companies to evade restrictions but are controlled by the foreign capital which made them possible. Very early, French, British, Belgian, German, and American capital poured into Spain. Spain at one time ranked first in the production of copper, but to-day she is sixth. In 1873, Spain sold her largest mines, the Rio Tinto, Zarza, and Tharsis, to an English company for 100,000,000 pesetas.

Os

The value of the wealth obtained since then by the English company is estimated at 23,000,000,000 pesetas.

A Frenchman founded the apricot pulp factory at Alicante in 1892. The Royal Asturian Company, controlling the zinc and lead mines, is Belgian. The C.H.A.D.E. (Spanish-American Electricity Distribution Company) was controlled by Belgian, French, American, and German interests. The Barcelona street railways used to make an annual profit of nine million pesetas for its Belgian owners.

During the World War, when growing Spanish industry experienced a boom period, foreign control also tightened its grip on it. German interests took control of acids and fertilisers through the Flix Electro-Chemical concern. The German I. G. Farbenindustrie gained control of dyes. The French controlled the Andalusian mines, Belgium the potash fields, and a combination of the Royal Bank of Canada and the French Compagnie Générale d'Électricité had a stranglehold on the Catalan electric trust. American capital has most recently been putting up stiff competition against the dominant British and French investors. Primo de Rivera gave the telephone monopoly to the International Telephone and Telegraph Company, which in 1930 yielded a profit of 34,300,000 pesetas. The 1935 report of the International Telephone and Telegraph Company stated that the investment of this company in the Compañia Telefónica Nacional de España amounted to over $48,000,000 and its total investment in Spain to $67,000,000.

According to Grosvenor M. Jones, Chief of the Finance Division of the U.S. Bureau of Foreign and Domestic Commerce, as reported by the Labour Research Association's *Economic Notes* of September 1936: " As of the end of 1933, total investments of United States long-term capital in Spain were estimated at $70,000,000. In all probability the total was not greatly changed at the end of 1935." Other estimates put the total American investment at close to $100,000,000.

A study of the direct investments of United States capital in various European countries issued in 1930 by the U.S. Department of Commerce gave eighteen manufacturing concerns in Spain with investments valued at nearly $12,500,000, nine oil companies with nearly $8,500,000 invested, and thirteen trading companies with an investment of over $4,000,000. The total investment in 1930 was estimated at $72,230,000.

The result of the sudden war prosperity was tremendous over-production for a country whose industry was still in its infancy. When the war ended, the economic vacuum was appalling. The balance of trade went minus again. The Catalan textile factories and the Basque mines were hard hit. Strikes swept Catalonia, and police and troops moved in the streets of the city. Machine guns mowed down workers in the Barcelona general strike of 1917, waged by the labourers for a portion of the war prosperity. With the end of the war, the boom collapsed, and labour " trouble " became a permanent fixture.

An extremely effective general strike broke out in Barcelona in 1919, during which, and for some time after, all constitutional guarantees were suspended and street fighting made the streets crimson. According to the semi-official government organ, *La Nación*, 337 people were killed and 434 were wounded in Barcelona Province alone in the year ending September 1923. In that month Primo de Rivera executed his " cold coup."

Primo de Rivera tried his utmost to put Spanish industry on its feet, even at the expense of agriculture. He raised the tariffs on industrial goods to an unprecedented height. He made some foreign-owned monopolies into government monopolies. He gave subsidies liberally wherever he thought they would do most good. In 1927 he created a Regulating Committee of Industrial Production to supervise Spanish industry. Most of Primo de Rivera's grandiose plan did little good. The world economic crisis of 1929 did not pass Spain by.

But Spanish industry suffered from a more basic

check upon its expansive powers. The serf-like condition of the peasantry and farm labourers holds mass purchasing power down to a minimum. The high cost of production in Spain, as well as foreign tariff barriers, forbids successful competition in the world market. The feudal landlords do not reinvest their profits, but squander their ground-rent abroad or in unproductive luxuries.

The precondition for industrial progress in Spain is a thoroughgoing agrarian revolution which will liberate the forces of production from the fetters of feudalism. This agrarian revolution has long been overdue and its nature is rooted deep in the history of Spain.

CHAPTER XV

PEOPLE WITHOUT LAND

A PROMINENT JOURNALIST, Cristóbal de Castro, wrote a book on Spain in 1931 of which the sub-title read: " A people without land and land without people."

This was the plight of Spain in its essence. Behind this aching and cutting indictment is the fact that of all the countries of Europe its population is spread thinnest, while at the same time the land is concentrated in the fewest hands.

Natives like to say that " Spain is a poor country." Some sections suffer from insufficient rainfall and others from parched earth and intense heat. Other countries have found ways of coping with these problems. And in *Das Kapital* Karl Marx says: " The secret of the flourishing state of industry in Spain and Sicily under Arab rule was to be found in irrigation works." However, even where natural conditions are most favourable, agricultural paralysis prevails. And the fact must not be overlooked that the most favoured regions are not the most productive.

The decline of Spanish economy became marked in the seventeenth century. When, in 1609, a million Moriscos, or Spanish Moors, were expelled, Spain lost her best agricultural workers. Back in mediæval days an all-powerful stock-raisers' corporation, the Council of the Mesta, was founded and given exclusive rights to an extensive " royal sheep-walk," from which area the people were rigidly excluded. An old book states that " starting from La Mancha and Estremadura in April, flocks of sheep annually ravaged Castile, returning in September to the places whence they came." The Mesta was only one of the ways by which the government discriminated against agriculture in favour of sheep-raising, to the detriment of the land. It lasted well into the nineteenth century. Wars of pillage, revenge, and intolerance brought nothing but misery for the people, and economic decline. At the same time feudal military grandees assumed ownership of vast tracts of land, the exploitation of which went to pay for their interminable wars and parasitic retinues.

The feudal economy was typically an economy of great landed estates, worked by peasants in return for obligations to the grandee in the form of services or payments in kind or money or both. The peasants were tied down to the land, generation after generation working the same parcel. Between the grandee and his peasants, there came a caste of overseers who acted as the social and economic intermediaries between the landlord and the land labourers. In practically all matters of importance to the peasant the grandee was all-powerful and the word of his retainers was law.

The feudal lords of Spain were, in many respects, even less efficient than the lords of the manors of feudal Europe in general. They permitted their estates to go completely uncultivated, especially in Andalusia and Castile. Sheep-raising took the place of land-cultivation to a large extent. Enormous tracts of land were reserved purely for hunting and for the breeding of wild bulls for sacrifice in the national sport.

Down to this day, Spanish agriculture has not yet succeeded in shaking off the palsy of the feudal regime. Only 40 per cent of the land is actually cultivated, and of this one fourth lies fallow annually. The latest figures for the amount of cultivated and uncultivated land in Spain are for 1932:

	Acres
Mountains and meadows . .	58,419,000
Barren land . . .	12,594,000
Towns and roads . . .	3,560,000
Cultivated lands . . .	50,234,000
of which	
Fallow land	12,401,000
Total area	124,807,000
Uncultivated	74,573,000
Cultivated	37,833,000

When it is said that the people of Spain " lack " land, some explanation and qualification is necessary. There is plenty of land, because Spain, next to France, is the largest country in Western Europe. There is not enough land for the masses of small peasants and farm labourers because of the form of ownership and division of the land. There is not enough, that is to say, unless land is taken from those who own more than they need or can cultivate.

Agriculture and fishing directly occupy 56·1 per cent of the people. More than a majority are occupied with agriculture alone. Statistics in Spain are very incomplete and only partially reliable, but they give some idea of the state of affairs. Here are the best figures:

In 27 out of 50 provinces registered in 1931 (the last complete land registration was made in 1881), 76·5 per cent of the people owned 4·7 per cent of the land, while 2 per cent owned 67 per cent of the land.

The regions suffering most from the great estates are Estremadura, Andalusia, and Castile. In twelve provinces of these three regions, 13 per cent of all the landowners are rated as large landowners, controlling 63·15 per cent of the land. Of the 758,952 landowners in the southern zone, 273,623 owned less than a hectare (2·471 acres), 291,623 from 1 to 5 hectares, and 82,517 from 5 to 10 hectares.

According to the data of the Institute for Agrarian Reform set up to study the land problem in 1932, not more than 100,000 out of the 800,000 families were provided with enough land to maintain themselves independently of other resources. Of the remaining 700,000, half were deprived of all land, and the other half had parcels so tiny that they were obliged to supplement their income by part-time wage-labour, or the full-time wage-labour of members of their households. There are provinces in which the great landlords owned half the land. There are provinces in which the great landlords owned two thirds of the land.

About one third of the land is under cultivation by the tenant or share-cropper system. Frequently tenants and sub-tenants are involved on one parcel of land so that middlemen appropriate part of the crop. Feudal dues ate up a large part of the produce. The peasants of Galicia, León, Asturias, and Zamora paid heavy feudal dues called " foros " and " subforos." The " rabacca morta " of Catlonia required the wine-growers to give the landlords as much as two thirds of the crop.

In Catalonia and on the Mediterranean coast, the chief land problem is not the huge estate, cultivated or uncultivated, but just the reverse. Here, instead of the great latifundia, the farms are pitifully small, altogether too small for profitable and efficient cultivation. The agrarian problem in

Spain is chiefly one of dividing up the great estates, but there is also a problem of the opposite extreme.

In the villages the cacique is a uniquely Spanish feudal political boss. The caciques are the stewards or agents of the landlords, although, in latter days, of the bankers and big business men too. He is the Spanish feudal equivalent of the ward boss, except that his powers are wider and greater. The caciques used to be able to swing municipal and parliamentary elections as the direct representatives of the most powerful interests in the community.

At first glance, the land problem is a stupendous one. It can only be compared and understood with reference to the land problem which prevailed in Russia under the tsars. The tenants are too poor to introduce farm machinery or modern instruments of cultivation. The extensive method of cultivation on the big estates is very wasteful. Irrigation systems are out of the question because there is nobody to pay for them and nobody to plan them.

As a result, Spain is a relatively unproductive country. The backwardness of agrarian technique reflects itself in the yield. The largest crop is wheat. The average yield per hectare in Europe in 1933 was 15·1 double cwt. In Spain the wheat yield was 10·5 double cwt. Both France and Spain are wine-producing countries. In 1933 there were 3,815,903 acres under vines in Spain, producing 521,461,958 gallons of wine. In France there were only

3,776,630 acres under vines; nevertheless, France produced almost double the amount of wine— 1,138,852,000 gallons in 1933.

So, despite the high Spanish birth-rate, the poverty of the people has kept the population down to the scantiest in Europe. Even France, notorious for its population problems, is more densely peopled. Spain averages 125 people per square mile, Portugal 192·3 people, France 196, Italy 344, Germany 363, and Great Britain 504.

That is how matters stood with the Spanish land problem right up until the 1933--6 period, when the peasants began to take things into their own hands, when the electoral victory of the People's Front brought some relief, and when the fascists took up an armed struggle against the Republic in order to keep any really thorough-going agrarian revolution from taking its course. Practically nothing was done to remedy this state of affairs under the monarchy, for the monarchy leaned upon the great landowners and the Church. How could it be otherwise? Land reform would have signalised the end of the monarchy.

One of the earliest proposals for land reform came before the First Republic. On June 22, 1874, José Maria Orense, a grandee who turned repub-lican and had an important hand in founding the Republican Party, introduced a bill into the Cortes for the division of uncultivated land among the landless. The bill did not get very far, but it indicated that far-sighted republicans even at that time understood Spain's most pressing problem in its essence.

Matters stood pretty much the same until de Rivera came into power. The dictator went through the motions of hastening the dissolution of the large estates in a royal decree of January 7, 1927. This law stated that tenants on land uncultivated by their owners could buy the plots upon which they were working. The joker in this decree is obvious.

When the Republic came in 1931, it foundered most badly on the land question, the key question of the revolution. Here the republicans came into direct collision with the Church and the grandees. Here they compromised most shamefully. Yet so long as the land question remained unsettled, republicanism was doomed, because reaction could always jump back into power at the first sign of crack-up. So long as their economic power remained intact, the landowning interests had nothing fundamentally to fear for their political power.

The republican Constitution said nothing concrete about expropriation, confiscation, or division. It was promised, however, that the government would take up the question shortly. During the summer of 1932 a proposed Agrarian Reform Law was discussed and finally passed by the Cortes on September 9, 1932—a year and a half after the Republic was proclaimed.

The provisions of the law broke sharply with the past. They were far-reaching, although not so fundamental as some desired, but they could have served as a decisive beginning in breaking the hold of the feudal latifundia upon Spain. The law stated that uncultivated land could be expropriated, together with the estates of exiled monarchists. All owners, except those of the feudal estates, were to be compensated. The expropriated land could be distributed either to individual tenants and labourers or to co-operatives, depending on the choice of communities. The law also completely abolished feudal dues, without indemnification. An earlier law, in January 1932, had confiscated all the property of the Jesuits. This latter law was supposed to go into effect on October 1, 1933.

Unfortunately, after delaying for a year and a half, the Republican-Socialist coalition then in power did not have the courage to take immediate and effective action. A year of " study " of the whole question was provided, so that, in violation of previous promises, the law did not begin to operate immediately.

The Republican-Socialist coalition which ruled Spain from 1931 to 1933, by postponing the day of reckoning with the semi-feudal landlords, cut its own political throat. Furious with the provisions of a law which meant their economic and social rout, the landowners bent every effort to return to power and it is, of course, in this period that the Popular Action and the C.E.D.A. of Gil Robles were organised. The Right reckoned better than the Left. In the autumn 1933 elections they returned to power. The economic implication of this reactionary victory was that the land-reform law was doomed.

Through a friendly Cortes the Lerroux Cabinet railroaded a new agrarian law which practically reversed the first. Without repudiating land reform entirely—that was impossible, considering the impatient and militant temper of the peasants—only fifty thousand pesetas were appropriated annually as compensation for expropriation. The conditions of purchase were so favourable to the grandees that they could have bankrupted the country in short order had they applied for " expropriation."

In any event, the land fund was a mere drop in the bucket, even if intended for use. The law immediately saved about 100 grandees with 1,400,000 acres of land from the threat of expropriation. The Lerroux government also backed a bill, offered by Robles's Popular Action Party, which returned all land expropriated without indemnification to its original owners. The Lerroux-Robles electoral

victory turned the economic clock back to the days
of the monarchy.

This reversal lasted until the February 1936
elections, when land reform went forward again,
faster than ever before, after the People's Front
victory. The Cortes passed a law on May 28, 1936,
calling for the re-examination of the cases of all
peasants expelled by the Lerroux-Robles government from the land for non-payment of rent. Many
thousands of peasant families were given the right
to return to the parcels of land they had rented
previously. Most important of all, as stated previously, about 100,000 peasants and their families
were actually settled on the land.

The 1936 fascist revolt, in this as in all matters,
was a desperate attempt by the landowners to
regain what was decisively threatened after the
February elections. A fascist victory would mean
the end of land reform. A People's Front victory
would mean the acceleration of land reform. In
the first days of the fighting the Giral Pereira
government declared that the property of the
landowners identified with the fascist cause was
confiscated. The religious orders were stripped of
their vast tracts.

Clearly, land for the peasants hinged upon the
outcome of the struggle.

CHAPTER XVI

CHURCH OVER SPAIN

THERE WAS one institution in Spain stronger than any man, mightier than any grandee or all of them, more powerful than the monarchy and more pervasive than the army.

That institution was the Catholic Church, with its religious orders. There are only 35,000 non-Catholics in Spain.

The Catholic Church was Spain's greatest landlord. It was also the most important industrialist, banker, schoolmaster, and money-lender. Its wealth has been estimated at one third of the national wealth. With monks, nuns, higher and lower clergy, it constituted a veritable army of occupation.

There is one priest for every 900 persons, compared with one for every 20,000 in Italy, the seat of the Papacy. All told, there are 106,734 persons either in the clergy or in the religious orders, 25,474 of them priests and 81,260 monks and nuns. In no other country did the clergy constitute such a disciplined and powerful vested interest. Only

Ps

a major operation on the body politic could dislodge them. This accounts for the statement of Margarita Nelken, the Left Socialist deputy that " in other countries the crowd, in a moment of national uprising, attacks banks and palaces, while here it burns convents and churches."

The Church has always directly intervened in the politics of the country through its own political spokesmen. It had its own Press, the best-equipped in the country. It took sides in every question of importance.

For centuries, more than the monarchy, the Church served as the real unifying centre of the country. It was the Christian princes who waged successful war against the Moors for eight long and bloody centuries. Rebellions were directed against the monarchy, but not against the Church. The disputants to power were all Catholics.

Like the land question, the religious question came up for settlement in Spain long after Europe as a whole had forgotten about it. In the mediæval period the Church, as a great landowner, entered into the complex of economic and social practices and institutions which made up the feudal system with decidedly earthly powers. This was true of Europe as a whole. The trouble with the situation in Spain is that the Church maintained its old feudal prerogatives right down to the present because the feudal system as a whole was so singularly long-lived. The Spanish Church is a semi-feudal Church, not at all as flexible as that in other countries.

While individual grandees lived and died, while feudal houses flourished and faded, the Church was a going concern which went on for ever, according to its trustees, the clergy. In the mediæval period, and long after, religiously-minded landowners frequently donated huge sums of money or large tracts of land to the Church in payment for absolution. The old feudal doctrine of mortmain, according to which the Church could only gain new lands, but could never surrender or lose what once she had, continued to be enforced right into the twentieth century.

The Church itself operated its lands and its wealth on a purely business basis, many times more efficiently than the grandees. As the richest landowner it employed thousands of farm-labourers. As the owner of latifundia it extorted huge sums in rent from its tenants. The religious orders, especially the Jesuits, showed great business enterprise in multiplying the profits from the land. They invested very profitably in industry, shipping, and banking and competed most successfully with the best lay enterprises.

The Jesuit order, for example, owned the Banco Urquijo in Madrid, with a capital of 126,000,000 pesetas. It controlled four smaller provincial banks with a total capital of 85,000,000 pesetas. The northern railway, orange groves in Andalusia, mines in the Basque Provinces and the Riff, factories in Barcelona were reported in their avowed or concealed control.

In rural districts the Church organised credit co-operatives, so that in the small peasant villages, the local clergy assumed the additional role of money-lender. In 1910 the Church organised the Consejo Nacional de las Corporaciones Católicas (National Council of Catholic Workers' Associations) as a Catholic union centre, especially for farm labourers in Castile, Estremadura, and Andalusia.

In no other country did the Church maintain such a monopoly over the " souls " of the people. Schools were always few, but monasteries and churches were many. What schools there were came under the control of the Church. Until 1857 education was practically the exclusive right of the Church. A law passed in that year to promote popular State education became a dead letter owing to clerical opposition. In 1931 at least half of the children in school were directly educated by the clergy, while both State and municipal schools also came under its supervision.

But the Church failed miserably in this, as in all other things. According to the latest census, made in 1930, 45·46 per cent of the population could neither read nor write. According to the 1930 census of the United States, only 4·3 per cent of the population could neither read nor write. In the middle of the nineteenth century, when the Church had a complete monopoly over education, only 20 per cent of the Spanish people were literate.

The essential reason why the power of the Church had to be broken by the Republic, if only for self-preservation, lies obviously in the tremendous economic, social, and political power exercised by the clergy. As the greatest landowner, the Church was naturally the foremost enemy of agrarian reform. To expropriate and divide the land meant, in the first place, to expropriate and divide the land of the Church. The Church could not avoid siding with those who wanted to preserve the old order of things if it wished to maintain its dominant position. But the Republic without land reform, educational reform, and political reform was an impossibility. By throwing itself athwart the path of progress, the Church inevitably forced its own ruin.

Until 1931 Church and State in Spain were not separated. Even the Constitution of 1812, which subordinated the monarchy to the Cortes, left the Church untouched. This Constitution stated without qualification : " The religion of the Spanish people is and shall be perpetually the Apostolic

Roman Catholic, the only true one. The nation protects it with wise and just laws and prohibits the exercise of any other."

Later, the relationship between Church and State was based on the Concordat of 1851. This agreement declared that " the Catholic Apostolic Roman religion, to the exclusion of every other cult, continues to be the sole religion of the Spanish nation and will be conserved always in the dominions of His Catholic Majesty with all the rights and prerogatives which it ought to enjoy according to the law of God and that ordained by the sacred canon."

Seventeen years later the provisional Constitution of 1868 made what amounted to a clean sweep of all Church privileges—on paper. The provisional government dissolved the religious orders, refused to make payments to the Church, and confiscated the property of the religious orders. But the clergy awoke in time to the great danger facing them, energetically entered the campaign of 1869, and gained the election of sufficient deputies to nullify the law. The Constitution introduced in 1869 obligated the State to maintain the Catholic religion. When Alfonso XII came to the throne in 1875, the Church returned just as purse-proud and powerful as ever.

The Catholic orders were suppressed four times in the nineteenth century, but they always came back. It has been characteristic of the Catholic Church in Spain that it has been able to outlive its bitterest foes, to overcome suppression, to snub all constitutional limitations, and to bulge with riches while the country as a whole was sinking into demoralising poverty.

When Primo de Rivera came to power in 1923, he leaned as much upon the Church as the Church did upon him. The slogan which he identified with his regime was: "Country, Monarchy, Religion."

How much the Church owed to him is shown by the following episode. In March 1929—Primo de Rivera resigned on January 28, 1930—a royal decree gave two Catholic institutions of higher learning, the Jesuit College at Deusto and the Augustine College at the Escorial, the right to issue their own diplomas and to set up their own examining boards. Prior to this time, outside of the eleven State universities, practically all private instruction was in the hands of the religious orders. The orders, however, were not permitted to grant academic titles or degrees. The right to give examinations for degrees was reserved to the State institutions. When the proposal to give the Church institutions power to issue their own diplomas, and thus to become virtually independent of the State, was placed before the National Advisory Assembly, it was rejected even by that dubious body after long and heated debate as reactionary. Nevertheless, it was put into effect, by royal decree. The Church had the monarchy and the dictatorship to thank for that. But it was riding for a fall.

When the constitution of the Second Republic was proclaimed, the Church structure began to crack. Church and State were separated and religious freedom was established. Divorces were permitted in civil courts, cemeteries were secularised, and the Church was no longer tax-exempt. Its subsidies were to be cut by one third in the budget of 1932 and to be cut off entirely after November 1933. In January 1932 the Cortes dissolved the Jesuit Order and confiscated its property. The religious orders were prohibited from buying property other than that intended for living and the practice of religion. The ecclesiastical corps with the army were dissolved. Subsequent legislation prohibited the clergy from participating in industry, commerce, and education.

The Vatican, accustomed to centuries of domination in Spanish affairs—the popes played an important political role in the nineteenth century —quickly struck back. The bishops of Spain issued a pastoral strictly forbidding attendance of children in State schools. In June 1933 Pope Pius XI issued a special encyclical protesting against the separation of Church and State. Members of the government were declared excommunicated.

The Republican-Socialist coalition in power at this time handled the Church question as it handled most other things. Its actions did not square with its words. The government did not confiscate more than a quarter of the Jesuit property. Dissolution of the orders and confiscation of the land were not scheduled to go into effect until October 1, 1933. Again the day of reckoning was postponed, with the same sad effects.

When October 1, 1933 rolled around, the Republican-Socialist coalition was no longer in power. The elections were being held just then, and as a result of these elections the Church came back into the saddle via Gil Robles's Popular Action Party.

Premier Lerroux almost immediately announced that his regime would not enforce measures prohibiting religious education, on the pretext that secular education was impossible. Pita Romero, a close henchman of Gil Robles, was put into the Foreign Ministry to patch things up with the Vatican. By turning the clock back on land reform, the Lerroux-Robles government saved the economic power of the Church. The religious orders were compensated for whatever had been taken away and their ruffled feelings were calmed.

After the February 1936 elections the pendulum swung the other way and the old laws were

re-enacted. The intervening period between the
February elections and the July revolt was comparatively short, however, and it was not until the
fighting had started that any drastic measures
were actually put into effect. On July 28, 1936 all
buildings and property of the religious orders were
confiscated by order of the Ministry of Education,
enforcing Article XXVI of the 1931 Constitution.

Unquestionably a People's Front victory had to
mean the completion of the 1931 revolution. What
the republicans did not accomplish of their own
volition the exigencies of civil war forced upon
them.

CHAPTER XVII

THE OFFICER CASTE

BEFORE the republican and labour movements became forces to be reckoned with, there were only two organised and homogeneous forces in all Spain. One was the Church. The other was the army.

There is no army in Europe like the Spanish army. It is unique in a number of respects. It was always defeated in foreign wars. It is the most inefficient and ineffective in modern history. Yet no other army ever played so important a role in the life of a nation. It has always been poorly provisioned and badly armed. Yet no other army consumed so large a proportion of the national income. It has repeatedly thrown itself athwart the will of the people. Yet when Napoleon invaded Spain, it was the people, not the army, that threw him out.

None of these pairs of facts are contradictory. They complement each other.

By 1898, after the disastrous war with the United States, Spain had been completely pushed out of the Americas, where once she had been the foremost conqueror. After that, all that was left of the once huge colonial empire were some small possessions in Africa, the most important of which was Spanish Morocco. The loss of her overseas possessions made a large proportion of her officers and men in service superfluous. The size of the armed forces did not, however, decrease to any appreciable extent.

Officers and men had literally no place to go. The tradition of the conqueror, the *conquistador*, was strong, but the opportunities for conquest were over. The army became a great cancer upon the country, bartering the freedom of the people for the status quo in the commanding staff. Whereas the army had before extended its baneful influence outward, now all of its activity had of necessity to turn inward, to Spain itself.

With the real beginnings of industrialisation after 1898, with the slow but certain development of the republican movement, the monarchy was more and more forced to depend upon the army as a buffer and a weapon against social unrest and economic change.

The main reason for the peculiar importance of the army was the desperate need of the monarchy, the Church, the landlords, and the big capitalists of sufficient support to cope with the growing discontent of the peasants, the republicans, the nationalists, and the proletariat. The more rotten the social and economic structure of the country became, the more insecure was the position of those who stood at the top of the structure. The danger of revolt made it unhealthy for the dominant powers to antagonise the armed forces.

The special and highly original organisation of the army fitted in nicely with the needs of the ruling interests for the greater glory of the officer caste.

In organisation, the Spanish army has always been notorious for two things: its numbers were ludicrously out of all proportion to the needs of the country; its officer force was ludicrously out of all proportion to the needs of the army.

In 1898 there were 499 generals, 578 colonels, and 23,000 other officers commanding an army of roughly 150,000 men. In 1913 there were 11,358 officers and 87,471 men in Spain, and 1,249 officers and 34,469 men in Morocco. The proportion of officers to soldiers was one officer for six to ten men.

This relatively huge officer class was favoured in yet another way. From two thirds to three quarters of the military budget, at least until 1931, was regularly allotted for salaries and sinecures to the officers, with the rest allotted to salaries for all the remainder of the army, together with provisions, armaments, materials, etc.

In 1898 the war budget ran as follows:

	Pesetas
Salaries for officers . . .	80,000,000
Salaries for troops . . .	45,000,000
Materials, armaments, munitions,	
etc.	13,000,000

This state of affairs continued right into 1931, when 490,000,000 pesetas were spent on salaries for the generals and other officers out of a total war budget of 651,000,000 pesetas. The pay for the lower ranks was a mere five pesetas a day. Only 161,000,000 pesetas were left for equipment and provisions.

As a result, Spain has always had an army within an army, or rather a caste within the army. This caste, maintaining rigid caste distinctions, was constituted of the officers. They were carefully recruited from the owning classes, from the nobility and the landowners. Very few were drawn from the ranks of the common people, few even from the middle class. The cavalry was especially a haven of reaction. Because it was not mechanised, it had none of the technical character which somewhat changes the class character of a large modern army.

Apart from the regular troops, there are other important armed formations. The Civil Guard, amounting to from 30,000 to 40,000 men, disciplined and well trained, the cream of the armed forces, was originally formed about one hundred years ago, to fight bandits. Since the World War it has been increasingly used against peasant unrest and labour strikes. The Civil Guard was always carefully maintained in complete isolation from the populace, removed from the cities and quartered in special garrisons.

The labour movement long clamoured for its dissolution. When the Republican-Socialist coalition came into power in 1931, practically nothing was done to satisfy this demand except through liberal promises. Another armed formation, the Assault Guard, was formed on the pretext that the Civil Guard was to be dissolved. The idea was to create a more republican guard than the Civil Guard had proved itself to be. It is true that the Assault Guard, many members of which were recruited from the unemployed, was much less reactionary than the Civil Guard. But the latter was not dissolved. And the officers of the Assault Guard were chosen from the Foreign Legion, the regular army, and the Civil Guard. A third special armed force was the Security Guard. The Carabineros, used as customs guards on the frontier, amounted to about 15,000 men.

The army got an early taste of power back in 1820 when several corps under General Rafael del Riego engaged in a temporarily successful revolt for the restoration of the Constitution of 1812. This was the first time in the nineteenth century that the army interfered in the politics of the country. It turned out successfully and it was, strangely enough, against the monarchy. The effects of the del Riego revolt were wiped out only two years later when a French army marched into Spain to restore the monarch, Fernando VII.

In 1835, for the second time in that century, the army forced the resignation of a high political figure, Martínez de la Rosa, President of the Council of Ministers. Later, in 1874, in the war against the Carlists, a rebellion in the army materially hindered the campaign against the Pretender's supporters, but discipline was sufficiently restored in the next year to permit the successful conclusion of the war.

Beginning in 1917, the army entered affairs of State as a decisive and deciding factor. An Officers' Junta was organised, ostensibly to protect their status, but actually to guide the fast-tottering monarchy. Under the Republic the old Officers' Junta gave way to the Spanish Military Union.

Never had an army been humbled more than was the army of Spain during the eighteen long years of the campaign to subjugate Morocco. It was the Moroccan scandal that touched off the fuse ignited in the de Rivera dictatorship of 1923.

One war against the Moroccans had been begun in 1859 and successfully terminated the next year. But the more recent war was a complete and ruinous disaster. Abd-el-Krim, leader of the Riff tribes, put up a stout defence with a paltry few thousand troops. The Moroccan sore finally came to a head with the famous disaster of Anual. The Riffs had been having all the better of the war when ten thousand men under General Fernández Silvestre engaged them and in July 1921 occupied the town of Igueriben, about a mile from the military post of Anual. Abd-el-Krim swooped down on the Spanish garrison and wiped them out with, it is said, the exception of seven men. General Silvestre himself was reported to have committed suicide in the slaughter.

The amount of money spent in the Moroccan fiasco could have paid for the economic reconstruction of Spain, said the first Finance Minister of the Republic, Jaïme Carner. According to him, the monarchy had squandered five billion pesetas in the last five years of the campaign. A special edition of *El Debate* of May 1929 gave the cost of the Moroccan campaign for eighteen years as approximately £160,000,000. For more than a decade Spain lost thirteen thousand soldiers annually against the elusive and courageous Riffs. The Moroccan budget from 1927 to 1929 devoted eighty-five per cent to the upkeep of the army and less than two tenths of one per cent for education, sanitation, and public works.

Two army revolts served as bloody omens of the
Q s

bloodless revolution of 1931. The first, in January and February 1929, was attempted by the Artillery Corps and inspired by José Sánchez Guerra, one-time President of the Chamber of Deputies and a far-sighted reactionary politician. Sánchez Guerra wanted to overthrow Primo de Rivera in order to save the monarchy. He felt that unless the Constitution was restored under the monarchy, it would not be long before a Constitution would be proclaimed without the monarchy. The plot was prematurely uncovered and failed completely.

The Jaca Revolt by Major Galán and Captain Hernández was a much more serious affair, but the timidity of the republican and Socialist leaders doomed it to failure.

Since the establishment of the Republic, army revolts have been uniformly reactionary. The most important one, prior to the 1936 uprising, occurred in August 1932, led by General José Sanjurjo—the same Sanjurjo who crashed to his death in a plane hurrying from Portugal to Spain in the early days of the 1936 uprising.

When the republicans assumed power in 1931, they realised that the army and the officer caste constituted one of their most urgent and difficult problems. So long as the top-heavy and parasitic officer caste was not brought under control, restoration and reaction would remain an over-hanging threat. The Socialist-Republican coalition made a characteristic compromise. They made drastic reductions in number, but the old order remained, reduced.

The so-called Law of Jurisdiction, which gave the army the right to court-martial any of its critics, was repealed. All officers were required to sign a pledge of loyalty to the Republic. The active officers' list was slashed from 26,000 to 7,662, plus 1,756 in service in Africa. The rest were put in the reserve. It was this discontented reserve that furnished the backbone of the 1932 Sanjurjo revolt. The number of military academies was reduced from five to two. The regular troops were cut to 105,367—still far too many for the country, but decidedly fewer than before.

The reactionary come-back late in 1933 practically negated all of these reforms. Republican and anti-fascist soldiers and officers were systematically weeded out. Hundreds of those who participated in the Sanjurjo affair were restored to their posts of honour. A decree was issued prohibiting workers in munition factories from joining trade unions.

By sending the leading generals into " exile " after the People's Front electoral victory in February 1936, the Left Republican government in power repeated its mistake of 1931–3. The Communists and Socialists pointed out the folly of sending Franco to the Canary Islands and Goded

to the Balearic Islands, but it did no good. The
" exiling " of the generals after February simply
pushed the date of their revolt slightly ahead.

The Spanish army, like the Spanish Church and
the Spanish agrarian problem, changed less in the
the last century than the corresponding institutions
in any other country in Europe. John Hay,
Abraham Lincoln's famous Secretary of State and
biographer, visited Madrid in 1870 and had some
keen things to say about the Spanish army of that
day. His words hardly need modification for our
own :

" In all nations, the engine which is most
dangerous to liberty . . . is the standing army. But
the army spirit of Spain is probably the worst in
the world. In other countries, the army is not much
worse than useless . . . but the Spanish army, from
general to corporal, is penetrated with the poison
of conspiracy. . . . Every successive minister has
used it for the purposes of his own personal ambi-
tion, and has left in it a swarm of superfluous
officers who owe their grades to personal or
political services, more or less illegal. . . . There
is scarcely a general in Spain but owes his successive grades to successive treasons."

CHAPTER XVIII

NATIONS WITHIN A NATION

IN MOST COUNTRIES the problem of national minorities is associated with economically backward regions. In Spain it is just the reverse. Its chief industrial and agricultural region has always been treated more like a colony than a province.

They say that if the people of Catalonia came to America they would become Americans, but if they settled in Madrid they would never become Castilians. Catalonia, richest and most productive region in all Spain, has always considered itself a nation apart. Its inhabitants are Catalans rather than Spaniards. To a somewhat lesser extent, that is also true of the Basque country and Galicia, where the national problem has become acute.

These three regions were able to guard and maintain their autonomist outlook because of the extremely late unification of Spain. Italy was once known as a " geographical expression," but Spain always deserved the epithet better. The great mountain ranges make natural self-contained regions. Before the coming of the railroad and the aeroplane these regions were effectively shut off from each other.

Catalonia appears as a national unit as far back as the beginning of the ninth century, when Charles Martel marched into the peninsula. The Catalans resisted these inroads upon their independence and maintained their autonomy until the twelfth century. During these centuries they developed a separate language, literature, and government. The Catalan language is quite different from Spanish and resembles the Provençal dialect of southern France. At one time, indeed, Catalonia belonged to France.

In the fifteenth century the Catalans were finally conquered by the Christian kings, occupied about that time with driving out the last of the Moors. But it was not until 1714 that a Spanish monarch, Felipe V, stripped the Catalans of their representative institutions. By the nineteenth century their liberties had all been taken away by the despotism which had its seat in the capital of Castile, Madrid.

The Catalans never forgot nor forgave, and they made periodic efforts to regain their independent status. When the Primo de Rivera dictatorship clamped an iron and bloody heel over the soil of Catalonia, the national question began to assume important proportions again. To-day it constitutes one of the most important elements in the headwinds of revolutionary Spain.

Catalonia consists of four provinces, Barcelona, Gerona, Lérida, and Tarragona, with a population of a little more than three million people. Catalans also live in the Balearic Islands, in parts of Aragon, and in a section of Valencia. French and Spanish Catalans combined number about five million.

Economic inequality has accentuated regional and historic differences. Catalonia never was held in the grip of the monarchy as tightly as was the rest of Spain. Industry had a better chance to develop. In mediæval days Barcelona, the chief city of Catalonia, was a commercial city-state on the style of Venice. Commercial capitalism was highly enough developed to fight off the enervating influence of the feudal decline which set in after the seventeenth century.

The province of Barcelona, the most important of the four Catalan provinces, has by far the densest population in all Spain. Catalonia produces about twenty per cent of the country's total agricultural output. The port of Barcelona is the most important in the country and handles one quarter of the total commercial traffic.

The big industry in Catalonia is textiles. About ninety per cent of the total Spanish output is produced in this region. The industry employs about two hundred thousand workers. Catalonia also produces fifty per cent of all Spanish chemicals and twenty per cent of the paper.

Yet even in this most advanced industrial region, accounting for twenty-five per cent of all Spanish industrial enterprises, vestiges of feudalism were very strong until very recently. The hated " rabacca morta " was a Catalan institution. The feudal landowning system took particularly heavy toll among the Catalan peasants, called *rabassaires*, most of whom do not own their lands outright, while their parcels of land are the smallest in Spain.

The industrial development of Catalonia accounts for the unusual importance of the proletariat in this region. Both the labour movement and the national movement are stronger here than anywhere else.

The first serious autonomous effort put forth by the Catalans in the nineteenth century goes back to the 1868 period, when a Barcelona junta issued a manifesto addressed exclusively to " Catalans." When the First Republic was proclaimed, the Catalans greeted it with undisguised enthusiasm, but they were soon disabused of any notion that it meant autonomy for them. In 1917 a rump Cortes convened in Barcelona, after the Catalan deputies had stalked out of the national Cortes in Madrid. Their demand for a greater measure of independence went unheeded.

Until 1918 the nationalist movement in Catalonia was in the hands of the rich bourgeoisie, organised in the Liga Regionalista (Regionalist League), dominated by Francisco Cambó, a big capitalist and landowner. In that year Cambó accepted a position as minister to the crown, an act which disillusioned many of his less fortunately placed followers, who were under the impression that they were fighting the monarchy.

The Catalan nationalist movement then split into a Left wing and a Right wing, with Cambó at the head of the Rights and Colonel Francisco Macía at the head of the Left-wing Esquerra Catalana (Catalan Left). The present leader of the Catalan Lefts is Luis Companys.

The monarchy, the Church, the landowners, and the Officers' Junta were all opposed to compromising with the Catalan movement. Social reaction coincided with bitter, irreconcilable opposition to the autonomist desires of the Catalans. In large measure this fact forced the Catalan Left to co-operate more and more with the labour movement, always sympathetic to the aspirations of the Catalans, to gain its own ends. When the fighting of 1935 broke out, the Catalan Left came over to the side of the Left Republican government and the People's Front, while Cambó's Liga Regionalista supported the fascists.

When Primo de Rivera came to power,

Catalonia immediately suffered. One of Primo de Rivera's first measures was to prohibit the use of the Catalan language in the schools, churches, and public meetings. He suppressed about thirty papers in Barcelona and dissolved hundreds of professional and educational institutions. Montjuich Prison became notorious for its Catalan " visitors."

The reaction against de Rivera's cruel treatment came when Colonel Francisco Macía, head of the Catalan Left, led a revolt against the dictatorship in 1926. It was a short-lived effort, lasting only three days. Later, in 1928, Barcelona was also implicated in the Ciudad Real revolt.

The Catalan nationalists by this time understood that they had to throw their lot in with the republicans and with labour in order to win autonomy for themselves. It was a case of help your neighbour and help yourself. The monarchy and the dictatorship meant national oppression as well as social oppression. The Republic held out the hope of national liberation as well as social liberation. This was clear when the Pact of San Sebastián, signed on August 17, 1930 by all the republican groups joining for the first time in a united front against the monarchy, included a plank for Catalan autonomy.

The Republic was finally established and the Catalans, after centuries of impatient and sometimes tumultuous waiting, demanded to come into their own. The Catalan Left under Macía did not wait upon ceremony, but proclaimed an independent Catalan Republic but a few hours after the Republic had been set up in Madrid. Macía assumed the post of " President of the Catalan Republic."

For the second time Macía wavered after five days of negotiation with the new President, Alcalá-Zamora. The Catalan Left was induced to accept something less than its full demands. Instead of an independent republic, united in a federal union on equal terms with the Madrid government, the Catalan government was to be known as the Generalidad, with provisional status only. In exchange Alcalá-Zamora promised that the next regularly elected Cortes would take under early consideration a special Catalan Statute, to be drafted in Catalonia and approved by plebiscite.

The Catalan Statute was in due time drafted and overwhelmingly approved by a plebiscite held August 2, 1931. Twelve days later it was presented to the Cortes for ratification. But the Cortes delayed and delayed. It did not get around to debating it until May 1932, and it did not approve the Statute until the following September.

The Catalan Statute defined Catalonia as an " autonomous region within the Spanish State." This was a vast improvement over the monarchy, but denied the claim for independence on a federal basis. Other provisions made Catalan the official language of the region except in official relations with the central government, in which Spanish was to be used. The Catalan Generalidad was to be composed of a Cortes, consisting of eighty-five members, President, and Executive Council. The President was to be elected by the Cortes. The first Catalan Cortes convened on December 9, 1932.

Many Catalans, especially those of the extreme Left, were unsatisfied with the Statute and resolved not to give up their fight for total equality with the government which they denounced as " Castilian." This dissatisfaction finally came to the surface on October 6, 1934, when the Catalan Left joined the northern revolt in Asturias and elsewhere against the Lerroux-Robles coalition. The new leader of the Catalan Left as well as head of the Generalidad was Luis Companys, who succeeded Colonel Macía in both positions when the latter died in 1933.

The revolt in Catalonia was smashed, after only one night of fighting, by General Batet, commander of the Barcelona garrison. The Catalan capitulation was really as much due to the timidity of the Catalan leaders as to the military opposition. The Generalidad wanted to overthrow the Lerroux-Robles government without paying the price for doing so. It issued no orders to arm the workers. The leaders of the Catalan Left actually prevented the arming of the workers almost everywhere. Had they armed them in 1934 as they did in 1936, the revolt would have had excellent chances of success.

The Lerroux-Robles regime took ample revenge both for the original Statute, which they had fought under the slogan " Unity of the Fatherland," and for the abortive Companys uprising. On December 14, 1934 the Cortes voted the indefinite suspension of the Catalan Statute. A provisional government was set up, with a Governor-General appointed from Madrid. Companys, as previously related, was tried and sentenced to thirty years' imprisonment.

Catalonia had reverted to the status of a colony and was in a more ignominious position than even under the Primo de Rivera dictatorship. Every vestige of popular government was taken away. Rifle rule was rampant. Even in the February 1936 elections the Madrid government went the length of decreeing that all Catalans entitled to vote had to present themselves at police stations for registration. Had the reactionaries returned victorious in the elections, many nationalist, republican, Communist, Socialist, and anarchist heads would have rolled. As it turned out, only a quarter of the Catalan voters obeyed the registration decree.

The People's Front electoral victory liberated the Catalans as it liberated the workers and peasants. The amnesty freed Companys and his followers. The status of broad autonomy and democratic rights was restored.

The Republican-Socialist coalition, which had given the Catalans a large measure of autonomy, did less nobly in respect to the two other national minorities of the Basques and the Galicians.

The Basques occupy four provinces, Biscay, Guipúzcoa, Álvara, and Navarra, with a total population of about 1,300,000. About 200,000 more live in southern France. Biscay ranks next to Catalonia as an industrial region.

The Basques surrendered their independence not without fierce and sometimes bloody struggles. Until 1875 they did not serve in the Spanish army. They always enjoyed special autonomy privileges, called " fueros." For a long time they collected their own taxes and paid a flat sum once a year to Madrid.

In the Basque country, far more than in Catalonia, the Church acted very flexibly. Instead of coming into direct collision with the nationalist movement, the Church supported it. The Basque clergy, for example, showed its nationalist good faith by withholding the tithes for its own benefit rather than for the central Church fund. That was good business and good nationalism.

The three chief political groups in this region are the so-called Traditionalists, or Carlists, and the Right and Left nationalists. The Carlists and the right-wing nationalists upheld the fascists in the 1936 revolt. The Basque Left fought with the People's Front.

When the Republic was proclaimed in 1931, the Catalans were on the alert, but the Basques were a bit more slow. They waited ten days, and then it was too late. The Republican-Socialist government, however, did promise them recognition, but never made the promise good.

In October 1934 the Basque nationalists participated in the fight against the Lerroux-Robles government, especially because heavy taxes had been imposed on them a few months previously by the Samper government. The Basque nationalists, small traders, artisans, workers, and peasants, fought for two days in the city streets and for two weeks in the mountains. The important mining region of Biscay was for a time entirely in the hands of the anti-fascist forces.

The national question also exists in Galicia, although in a less pressing form than in Catalonia and the Basque Provinces. This region is also made up of four provinces, La Coruña, Lugo, Orense, and Pontevedra, with a total population of 2,275,000 people. There are also Galicians in Portugal, and their language strongly resembles

Portuguese. The remnants of feudalism are stronger here than anywhere else in Spain, and industry plays practically no role. Galicia is noted for its cattle and wheat and for the small subdivisions of land owned—a typical anomaly.

Between Galicia and Castile there has been strong antagonism because the Castilian landlords, anxious to get the highest possible prices for their wheat, established high national tariffs on imported corn. Because their cattle must be fed on corn, the Galician peasants were forced to raise their own corn and buy expensive Castilian wheat.

The Galician nationalists also formulated their demands for autonomy in 1931, but nothing came of it. The rising tide of the Catalan and Basque revolt, however, has kept the Galician question alive and the movement for autonomy growing.

CHAPTER XIX

THE LABOUR MOVEMENT

THE SPANISH LABOUR and revolutionary movements have deeply-rooted traditions which extend
back into the middle of the last century.

Starting with 1840, labour organisation made its
appearance on a very local and limited scale and
with vague objectives. Very little is certain of
actual forces and tendencies until the year 1868,
when a Barcelona machinist, Antonio Marsal
Anglora, made his appearance at the third Congress of the International Workingmen's Association, held in Brussels, September 6–15, 1868. This
International later came to be known as the First
International and is the direct forerunner of the
Labour and Socialist (Second) International and
the Communist (Third) International. Its chief
figures were Karl Marx and Frederick Engels.

Just a few months prior to its Brussels Congress,
the First International was joined by the great
anarchist and apostle of Panslavism, Mikhail
Bakunin, who intended to capture the organisation
by " boring from within." Bakunin did not press

Rs

his viewpoint before the Brussels meeting, but the
entire organisation soon became a battleground
in which a great struggle was waged between the
socialist ideas of Marx and Engels and the anarchist
views of Bakunin.

Every country became an arena for the conflicting philosophies, and Spain was no exception.
What was peculiar about Spain was that the
followers of Bakunin soon gained and kept the
upper hand. This early ascendancy of the anarchists
shaped the entire course of the Spanish labour
movement.

The foundation of the First International in
Spain was actually laid by an Italian follower of
Bakunin, José Fanelli. Fanelli organised the first
branch of the International, numbering twenty-
one people, in 1868, and the branch began to
function on December 21, 1868 in Madrid. More
branches were soon organised in Madrid and
Barcelona, and by 1870 the International claimed
15,000 members in 153 sections.

Barcelona from the very beginning was the
stronghold of the anarchists: there were in Barcelona more than three times the number of
members there were in Madrid, which was
dominated by Marxists. It has been claimed by
the anarchists that they could count on from
50,000 to 70,000 members in Spain in the early
'seventies.

Engels himself occupied the position of Corresponding Secretary for Spain but he seems early to have recognised the supremacy of the Bakuninists: he wrote in a letter of February 1870 that " Italy and Spain will have to be left to him [Bakunin], at least for the present."

The conflict between the two factions came to a head in 1871, when Paul Lafargue, later the son-in-law of Marx, fled to Spain as a refugee after the fall of the Paris Commune. Lafargue found the International dominated by the anarchists and soon forced a show-down. In that year there came into existence two organisations in Spain, one Marxist, the other anarchist, both claiming to be the official representatives of the international body.

The Bakuninists were finally expelled from the International at the 1872 Congress at The Hague. The Spanish section was split, with the bulk of the membership going with the anarchists. Of the five Spanish delegates at the Hague Congress, four were anarchists. The fifth, Lafargue, was barely admitted when the other four attempted to discredit his credentials.

Bakunin immediately set up his own International, and the Spanish section was undoubtedly the strongest link in the anarchist chain. The anarchists, however, were organisationally negligent and failed to keep their movement going on a solid foundation for very long. In 1881 they reorganised as the Federación de Trabajodores de la Región Española (Federation of Workers of the Spanish Region) of the International Working-men's Association, but the Federation lasted only until 1888.

The Socialist movement, meanwhile, grew slowly and it was not until May 2, 1879 that the Partido Democrático Socialista Obrera (Workers' Social Democratic Party) was formed. Its outstanding personality was Pablo Iglésias, a printer by trade. The Socialists did not establish an official organ until 1888, when *El Socialista* was founded. In the next year, under Socialist inspiration, the Unión General de Trabajodores (General Workers' Union) was established. The union started with 3,000 members, grew to 26,000 in 1900, 42,000 in 1910, and 112,194 in 1915.

The differences between anarchism and socialism in this earlier period are still, in their essence, valid to-day. The anarchists opposed government of any kind, making no distinctions between a capitalist government and a workers' government. Both were equally reprehensible in their eyes. It is for this reason that in 1933 they permitted the Lerroux-Robles coalition to come into power by abstaining from the election.

In the economic field the anarchists despised strikes for partial and immediate ends on the theory that workers who won a little improvement would be discouraged from fighting for fundamental change. The anarchists worshipped the general strike as the infallible remedy for every abuse.

The early Socialists belong to the classical reformist school of peaceful and legalistic gradual change which would one day bring the workers socialism. They differed fundamentally from the anarchists in not taking a nihilistic view of government, and therefore waged electoral campaigns. They also differed from the later Communists in that their outlook was mainly parliamentary and they did not envision or support a revolutionary struggle for power in which the capitalist State would be destroyed and a workers' State established.

In the trade-union sphere the anarchist-led C.N.T. and the Socialist-led U.G.T. competed with each other and often clashed on tactics and principles. To the Socialist, the anarchists were hopelessly irresponsible and dangerously romantic. To the anarchists, the Socialists were criminally opportunist and camouflaged capitalist politicians of the Left.

The Socialist Party nominated its first candidate for office in 1891 and polled 5,000 votes. In 1910, thanks to a coalition with the Republicans, Iglésias was elected to the Cortes from a Madrid constituency. In 1918 the Socialist Party elected six members to the Cortes.

The youngest of the important working-class parties is the Communist Party. This party was founded after the national convention of the Spanish Socialist Party voted, on April 9, 1921, against affiliation with the Communist International by a vote of 8,805 against 6,025. It is clear that under the impact of the Russian Revolution there was a decided drift to the Left among the Spanish Socialists. The majority at the 1921 national convention voted to support the so-called Vienna or Second-and-a-Half International, but as a Party joined the Labour and Socialist (Second) International when it was revived some years later.

After the April 1921 Congress the minority split away and formed the Spanish Communist Party as the Spanish section of the Communist International. In 1923 the Communists were driven into complete illegality by the Primo de Rivera dictatorship. Only the Socialists were tolerated, and they were even encouraged by Primo de Rivera. Francisco Largo Caballero, even at that time a prominent Socialist, was a member of the dictator's Privy Council, Manuel Llaneza, another Socialist leader, became a member of the government's Fuel Commission, and Trifon Gomez joined the Railway Board.

The Communists did not emerge into open and

legal activity again until 1931, when their opposition to the activities of the Republican-Socialist coalition in power earned them a sort of semi-legal existence. They also suffered from inner party dissension and not until 1932–3 did they really become a unified party. Since then, they have played an important part in the affairs of the country, and to-day that part has become decisive.

Some of the groups which at one time or another were expelled from the Communist Party managed to maintain an independent existence. The followers of Leon Trotsky, led by Andrés Nin, were long more influential than the Communists, as were the " Right opposition " group led by Joaquin Maurin. Trotsky has, more recently, denounced both Nin and Maurin, who, with their influence fast waning since the October 1934 revolt, have joined together in the P.O.U.M. Their influence is limited almost solely to Catalonia.

The anarchists, after their early development in the 'sixties and 'seventies of the last century, reached a stalemate until the entrance of French syndicalism into the Spanish scene. With a common ground of opposition to all government and political action, the anarchist and syndicalist movements naturally fitted together. With the anarchists as its organising core, the syndicalist Confederación Nacional de Trabajo (National

Confederation of Labour) was founded in 1910. The anarchist movement of Spain and Portugal united in 1927 to form the Federación Anarquista Ibérica (Iberian Anarchist Federation). Although the anarchists and syndicalists still maintain separate organisations, their membership overlaps; the leadership of the C.N.T., however, is practically all anarchist. The chief strength of the C.N.T. is in Catalonia, Aragon, Andalusia, Valencia, and Alicante. At its Saragossa Congress, held in May 1936, it reported a membership of 600,000. Just before the fascist revolt the official figure had jumped to 700,000. The C.N.T. claims leadership of 1,000,000 workers, including many unorganised.

The U.G.T. is credited with about as many members. Its organisational strength is centred in Old and New Castile, the Basque country, and Estremadura. Within the last year, the Socialist-led U.G.T. merged with the Communist-led Unitary General Confederation of Labour. This merger greatly increased the strength of the united trade-union movement among the unorganised. The unified U.G.T. is to-day led by Communists and left-wing Socialists.

Since the February 1936 elections a strong movement for the unification of the Socialist and Communist parties has got under way, and important results have already been achieved. The Communist and Socialist youth movements have merged into one organisation with fraternal affiliation with the Young Communist International. The amalgamation was in process just when the fascist uprising broke out. As a result of the merger, the Socialist-Communist youth organisation has made tremendous gains in membership and influence. Prior to the February elections the Socialist youth numbered 24,000 and the Communist youth 14,000. At the time of the amalgamation the Socialist youth had increased its membership to 65,000 and the Communist youth to 50,682. Two weeks after the merger it was announced that the new organisation had a membership of 140,000.

In Catalonia the Socialist and Communist parties, together with the Proletarian Party, united into one organisation called the Unified Socialist Party of Catalonia, affiliated with the Communist International. This unified party has grown, but it is still weaker than the anarchists. Since 1933, great changes have also taken place in both the Socialist and the anarchist movements.

After the failure of the Republican-Socialist coalition government of 1931–3 a Left wing arose within the Socialist Party which soon comprised the great majority of the party. The outstanding leader of the Left Socialists is Francisco Largo Caballero, of whom it has been said that the whole working-class movement would have profited immeasurably had he begun to read the works of Lenin ten years earlier.

There were also Right and Centre groups in the Socialist Party, the first led by Julian Besteiro, a professor of logic, and the second by Indalecio Prieto. It was Besteiro who in 1915 introduced a resolution in the Socialist Party Congress for support of the Allies. The resolution was voted down 4,090 to 1,218.

In alliance with the Besteiro faction, Prieto to-day is chairman of the National Committee of the Socialist Party, although the rank and file are known to be overwhelmingly behind Largo Caballero. Prieto has never been too scrupulous about inner party politics. A special convention was scheduled for June 1936. It was obvious that Largo Caballero had the necessary strength to take over the party machinery. By a sudden coup, in which the vacant places were filled by " safe " men, the National Committee in May suddenly decided to postpone the Congress until October. Prieto hoped by that time to jump into the premiership and perhaps out of the Socialist Party. Largo Caballero protested against the manœuvre bitterly and called it dishonest.

The anarcho-syndicalists paid a heavy penalty for their abstention in the 1933 elections by loss of influence after the October 1934 uprising, because they recommended that all unions affiliated with the C.N.T. remain passive in the struggle. A number of anarchist leaders slowly began to shift from their traditional position, especially Angel Pestaña, one of the oldest and most prominent. The syndicalist rank and file meanwhile was plainly not going to abstain in another election and again let the reactionaries in through the crevices of the working-class front.

The issue became so acute that the National Committee of the C.N.T. was forced to issue a statement on its attitude in the event of new elections. This statement, published in *Solidaridad Obrera* on January 27, 1935, tried to justify the anti-political policy of the anarchists in the 1933 elections and again affirmed the organisation's attitude against participating in elections. "Tyranny and crime are equally deserving of condemnation, no matter whether they exist under the red-yellow flag of the monarchy or in the name of the tricolour of the Republic or even under the red banner of the dictatorship of the proletariat," read the statement.

But when the elections of February 1936 were held, thousands of anarchists in Catalonia and elsewhere disobeyed orders and flocked to the polls to vote for candidates of the People's Front. Gil Robles himself gave the anarchist vote as one of the reasons for the electoral victory.

The Saragossa Congress of the C.N.T. in May

1936 further emphasised the shift in doctrine made
by the anarchists. Largo Caballero, who was one
of the speakers, extended a friendly hand for trade-
union unity. This also represented a radical departure for Largo Caballero, because it signalised
his recognition of the importance of winning over
the syndicalists to joint action.

In the heat of the 1936 fighting the anarchists,
Socialists, and Communists of Catalonia formed a
" Liaison Committee " fo. joint action. When the
anarchists agreed to take this step, they broke a
long tradition of isolation and hostility to the other
working-class parties. An agreement was drawn up
as a basis for the work of the " Liaison Committee," and this document may determine the
future history of Spain. The agreement reads:

" In order to render the revolutionary action of
the workers against fascism more efficient, and to
reinforce and direct the current of unity created in
the battles on the 19th and 20th of the past month,
a Liaison Committee is constituted as of this date,
to consist of two representatives of the National
Confederation of Labour, two of the General
Union of Workers, one of the Iberian Anarchist
Federation, and one of the Unified Socialist
Party.

" First: This committee's mission will be to find
points of coincidence between these organisms,
submitting them to discussion, and for their

approval, in order to issue the proper slogans and directions afterwards.

" The creation of this committee in no way limits the individuality of the component organisations.

" When the signatory organisations reach an agreement on any point after previous discussion, the Liaison Committee will be responsible for seeing that each organisation's representatives in the various committees (Central Committee of Militias, Economic Committee, etc.) carry out the points of agreement between the organisations.

" The Liaison Committee will meet regularly three times each week and such other times as, in the judgment of participating organisations, shall be deemed necessary.

" This committee will propose to advise its members and organisations to form factory committees in all places of work, with proportional representation between the members of the U.G.T. and the C.N.T.

" The creation of this committee implies mutual respect between the unions and the freedom of the workers to join one of the two trade-union federations.

" While this committee exists, the component organisations agree to renounce all violent attacks and violent criticism. The criticism that may be reciprocally levelled must be completely fraternal.

" The committee will give a note to the Press announcing its constitution and informing the workers and public opinion in general of its objectives.

" This Liaison Committee will address itself to the National Committee of the C.N.T. and the Executive Committee of the U.G.T. informing them of this agreement and urging that the same be accomplished on a national scale."

The two leading Communists in Spain are José Diaz, general secretary, and Dolores Ibarruri, otherwise known by the glamorous name La Pasionaria. Diaz is a comparatively young man, with the best years of his life still before him. His father was a baker, and his mother a tobacco worker in Seville. He joined the Communist Party in 1927 and became the leader of the party in 1932. With Largo Caballero, he is the strongest man in the labour movement.

La Pasionaria is the daughter of a miner. As a young girl, she worked as a servant in the house of a rich family and later became a waitress in a café. She received no formal schooling, but joined the Socialist Party in Biscay at the age of seventeen. She is an exciting figure and moves audiences to tears and tumult. During the 1936 fighting she visited the Guadarrama front daily, cheering the soldiers to greater efforts.

The Spanish labour movement has been steeled in years of dictatorship and terror, and has overcome all defeats and obstacles with tremendous resourcefulness. Its future was never brighter.

CHAPTER XX

CONCLUSION

THE SPANISH CIVIL WAR of 1936 is the first social conflict in modern times in which the organised forces of reaction and the most powerful vested interests were forced into a position where they had no other resort than to take up arms against the legally established government. In Germany and Italy, fascism captured State power and used the entire machinery of the State against the democratic and revolutionary opposition. Spanish fascism sought to do likewise in the Lerroux-Robles period from 1933 to 1935. It failed. Soon it was too late.

In this respect Spain has set an important, and perhaps epochal, precedent. The democratic government could rally around it all those who supported constitutional rule as well as those whose main aim in the conflict was the fight against fascism. The insurgent character of the fascist bid for power automatically narrowed its popular support. When the government succeeded in gaining a breathing-space against the unquestionably superior initial military strength of the rebels, this became an important factor.

The People's Front was formed for just such a contingency. According to its ablest proponents, the People's Front was a coalition of democratic, labour, and revolutionary forces against the over-hanging threat of fascism. In terms of social classes, it signified an anti-fascist alliance between the middle class and the Left workers' and peasants' movement, including the revolutionary parties. Sad experience had emphasised for the Left, in Germany and Italy, that the middle class does not play an independent role in social conflict, but rather, in times of extreme social tension, allies itself cither with the revolutionary Left or with the fascist Right, with the workers or the biggest capitalists and landowners. In every case where fascism has triumphed, a section of the middle class has served as the social reservoir from which the fascists have recruited their storm-troop forma-tions and their popular support.

The alternative to the People's Front was thus plain. With the anti-fascist forces split, the extreme Left would be isolated, the middle class would hang in the balance and tend toward the extreme Right, with the fascist forces confident and on the offensive. With the People's Front firm, fascism could only come to power after a war of extermin-ation.

Ss

The old alternative of bourgeois republic and proletarian dictatorship did not face the extreme Left, such as the Communists and Socialists, either when the revolt broke out or during the conflict in any real sense. To have remained neutral between the Second Republic and the threat of fascism would have ensured the victory of the fascists. The post-February government would immediately have crumbled without the militant, decisive, and instantaneous support of the working-class Left. Conversely, the working class was certainly not strong enough to win in isolation. Everywhere but in Catalonia the industrial workers are in an extremely small numerical minority, and Catalonia under the best of circumstances could not stand alone for long.

The working-class parties did not adopt a policy of fighting against both the fascists and the democratic Republic simultaneously because such a policy, in terms of its consequences, denoted political suicide. The fascists were actually forced to falsify the issues in many regions, especially in Spanish Morocco, to get support. The Moors were recruited for war on the mainland with the story that an extremist revolt had broken out against the constitutional government. In many cases, when the falsification was uncovered by the insurgent recruits, unrest and desertions followed.

Equally important to understanding the unanimity with which all the progressive forces rallied to the side of the democratic Republic is the circumstance that " the immaculate revolution " of 1931 had been far from fulfilled. In the first two years of its existence the reigning Republican-Socialist coalition government had made far-reaching verbal promises, but much less significant concrete achievements. Yet Spain was so backward in comparison with the rest of Europe that half-way measures were out of the question. The real indictment of the 1931–3 government is not merely that it did not do enough, but that anything less than enough in the way of social and economic transformation was doomed to sterility. The social basis inherited from the monarchy was too rotten for the building of a democratic superstructure.

The Lerroux-Robles " counter-revolution " swept even these pale achievements into the discard. The dead arose to plague the living. Though the Right was in turn swept out in February 1936, the period between February and July, when the revolt broke out, was too brief for any really fundamental and thorough regeneration of the 1931 Constitution. Yet this Constitution offered the real possibility of making a clean break with the grandee, clerical, semi-feudal past. This was richly worth fighting for, even from the point of view of the extreme Left.

The People's Front held firm and even strengthened during the Civil War not only for the negative
reason that to break it would have opened the
social dikes to the fascist flood, but for the positive
reason that the struggle for the fulfilment, for
gathering the full fruits of the democratic revolution, was an absolute necessity.

Forged in the fire of civil war, a new Spain had
to emerge. A fascist Spain meant that a new ally
for Italian and German fascism had arisen out of
the ashes of the Second Republic. Like its pre-
decessors, the powerful trade-union movement,
both syndicalist and Marxist, would be smashed,
the democratic and labour parties outlawed, and
all civil liberties made a thing of the past for the
majority. France would be encircled by the Nazis,
the Spanish fascists, and the ocean. The political
physiognomy of the entire world of necessity had
to change.

The victorious Republic would necessarily be
very different from the Republic of the past. The
fact that the middle class could no longer be
subjected to pressure and influence from the
extreme Right would in itself serve to force it more
to the Left. Most to gain, however, had the poorest
and humblest layers of society. The peasants
would throw off the ancient shackles of the great
estates, if for no other reason than that the grandees
sided with the rebels and suffered confiscation

of their property in the early days of the strife.

The greatest transformation of all would take place among the working-class and revolutionary parties. The tendency towards working-class unity would be extremely powerful, and the organisational unification of the Socialist and Communist parties, even during the fighting, was on the order of the day. This unity was prepared by the unification of the Communist-led and Socialist-led trade-union movements into the unified General Workers' Union, by the organic unity of the Communist and Socialist youth movements, and by the amalgamation of the Socialist and Communist parties of Catalonia. This last development significantly coincided with the fascist revolt.

Achievement of Communist-Socialist unity would not yet heal the split in the working class, because of the presence of a strong and deeply-rooted anarcho-syndicalist movement. Coincident with the drive for Socialist and Communist unity had to come the effort toward the unification of the trade-union movement through the amalgamation of the General Workers' Union and the syndicalist National Confederation of Labour. Much has been achieved in this direction, but much remains to be done.

The fulfilment of pre-requisites such as these opens the way for far-reaching and even revolutionary changes in the Spain of the future. The

Communists and Socialists never surrendered an iota of their ultimate goal, notwithstanding the fact that their policies realistically were based upon the possibilities inherent in the actual moment. For both these parties ultimately, only a completely new social order based upon socialised production can transform a victory of the 1936 Civil War into an irrevocable Socialist victory.

Out of the carnage and wreckage of civil war, a new Spain had to emerge. The choice lay between the brutalising and violent enslavement of fascism and the liberating, progressive developments which a democratic victory could make possible.

GLOSSARY OF NAMES

Abd-el-Krim: leader of Riff rebellion in Spanish Morocco; exiled in 1926 to island of Reunion, near Madagascar.

Alcalá-Zamora, Niceto: reactionary; president of Provisional Government [1]; elected first President of Second Spanish Republic, December 10, 1931; impeached, April 7, 1936.

Alfonso XIII: last King of Spain (May 17, 1888 to April 14, 1931).

Alvarez del Vayo, Julio: Socialist; former Minister to Mexico; Foreign Minister since September 4, 1936.

Alvaro de Albornoz: republican; Minister of Public Works in Provisional Government.

Anastasio de Gracia: Socialist; Minister of Commerce and Industry since September 4, 1936.

Ascaso, Francisco: anarchist; killed in first days of 1936 Civil War.

Azaña, Manuel: leader of Republican Left; Minister of War in Provisional Government; Premier from October 1931 to September 1933 and from February 19, 1936 to May 10, 1936; elected second President of Republic, May 10, 1936.

Aznar, Juan: monarchist admiral; last Premier under monarchy (February 18, 1931 to April 13, 1931).

Batet, Domingo: fascist general; leader of 1936 fascist revolt.

[1] The Provisional Government lasted from April 14, 1931 until June 29, 1931. Alcalá-Zamora resigned in October 1931, before being re-elected on December 10.

Berenguer, Dámaso: monarchist general ; Premier under monarchy (January 30, 1930 to February 18, 1931).

Besteiro, Julian: leader of Socialist right wing ; former Speaker of the Cortes.

Cabanellas, Miguel: fascist general ; leader of 1936 fascist revolt, in command at Saragossa garrison.

Calvo Sotelo, José: monarchist-fascist ; Minister of Finance during Primo de Rivera dictatorship ; assassinated, July 13, 1936.

Cambó, Francisco: leader of Catalan Regionalist League.

Carillo, Santiago: secretary of united Communist-Socialist Youth League.

Carner, Jaïme: Catalan Left ; former Minister of Finance.

Casares Quiroga, Santiago: leader of former Galician (republican) Federation ; now with Republican Left ; Minister of Marine in Provisional Government ; former Minister of Interior and Public Works ; Premier (May 13, 1936 to July 18, 1936).

Chapaprieta, Joaquin: conservative ; Premier (September 25, 1936 to December 9, 1936).

Companys, Luis: leader of Catalan Left ; President of the Catalan Generalidad.

Diaz, José: general secretary of the Spanish Communist Party.

Durruti, Buenaventura: anarchist leader.

Fanjul, Joaquin: fascist general ; leader of 1936 fascist revolt ; executed, August 17, 1936.

Franco, Francisco: fascist general ; Chief of Staff during Gil Robles War Ministry ; leader of 1936 fascist revolt.

Galán, Fermín: army captain ; co-leader of republican Jaca Revolt, December 12, 1930 ; executed, December 14, 1930.

Galarza, Angel: Socialist; Minister of the Interior since September 4, 1936.

García Hernández, Angel: army captain; co-leader with Fermín Galán of Jaca Revolt; executed, December 14, 1930.

García Oliver, Juan: anarchist leader.

Gil Robles, José Maria: fascist; leader of Popular Action Party and C.E.D.A.[1]; Minister of War (May 6, 1935 to December 9, 1935).

Giner de los Riós, Bernardo: Republican Union; Minister of Communications since September 4, 1936.

Giral Pereira, José: Republican Left; former Minister of Marine; Premier (July 18, 1936 to September 4, 1936).

Goded, Manuel: fascist general; leader of 1936 fascist revolt in Balearic Islands; executed, August 12, 1936.

Goicoechea, Antonio: fascist; former monarchist; leader of Renovación Española.

Gonzalez Peña, Ramón: Socialist; one of the leaders of the October 1934 Asturian revolt.

Hernández, Jesús: editor of *Mundo Obrero,* central organ of Spanish Communist Party; Minister of Education since September 4, 1936.

Herrara Orio, Angel: clerical fascist; director of *El Debate,* clerical organ; backer of Gil Robles; organiser of National Action (Acción Nacional) in 1932.

Ibarruri, Dolores: Communist; known as "La Pasionaria."

Iglésias, Pablo: founder of Spanish Socialist Party and General Workers' Union.

Jiminez Asuá, Luis: Socialist.

Just, Julio: Republican Left; Minister of Public Works since September 15, 1936.

Largo Caballero, Francisco: leader of Socialist left wing; secretary of General Workers' Union; former Minister of Labour; Premier since September 4, 1936.

[1] See list of parties, following.

Lerroux, Alejandro: reactionary; leader of Radical Party; Minister of Foreign Affairs in Provisional Government; four times Premier between October 1933 and September 1936; ally of Gil Robles in 1934–6.

López de Ochoa, Eduardo: reactionary general.

Macía, Francisco: founder of Catalan Left; first President of Catalan Generalidad; died, December 1933.

March, Juan: capitalist; financier of fascist movements.

Martínez Barrios, Diego: leader of Republican Union; formerly with Radical Party; Minister of Economy in Provisional Government; Speaker of the Cortes since March 16, 1936; Premier for eight hours on July 18, 1936.

Maura, Miguel: reactionary; leader of Conservative Party; Minister of Interior in Provisional Government.

Maurin, Joaquin: co-founder of P.O.U.M.

Menéndez, Teodomiro: Socialist.

Mola, Emilio: fascist general; leader of 1936 fascist revolt in Old Castile.

Negrin, Juan: Socialist; Minister of Finance since September 4, 1936.

Nin, Andrés: co-founder of P.O.U.M.

Pestaña, Angel: anarchist leader.

Piera, José Tomás: Catalan Left; Minister of Labour since September 4, 1936.

Portela Valladares, Manuel: independent Right; Premier (December 30, 1935 to February 19, 1936).

Prieto, Indalecio: leader of centrist faction in Socialist Party; Minister of Finance in Provisional Government; former Minister of Public Works; Minister of Air and Marine since September 4, 1936.

Primo de Rivera, Miguel: fascist military dictator (September 13, 1923 to January 28, 1930).

Primo de Rivera, José Antonio: fascist; leader of Falange Española; son of Miguel Primo de Rivera.

Quiepo de Llano, Gonzalo: fascist general; leader of 1936 fascist revolt ; in command of Seville garrison.

De los Ríos, Fernando: Socialist; Minister of Justice in Provisional Government; former Minister of Education.

Romanones, Count de (Alvaro Figueros de Torres): monarchist; three times Premier and seven times Cabinet Minister under monarchy.

Ruiz Funes, Mariano: Republican Left; former Minister of Agriculture; Minister of Justice since September 4, 1936.

Saborit, Andrés: Socialist.

Samper, Ricardo: Basque Nationalist Party; Premier (May 2, 1934 to October 1, 1934).

Sánchez Guerra, José: liberal monarchist.

Sanjurjo, José: fascist general; leader of 1932 reactionary revolt; died in plane crash near Lisbon, Portugal, July 20, 1936.

Uribe, Vicente: Communist ; secretary of Communist fraction in Cortes; Minister of Agriculture since September 4, 1936.

GLOSSARY OF PARTIES

LEFT

Republican Left: Left petty-bourgeois party; strongly democratic; anti-fascist, anti-clerical; for progressive social reforms.

    Leader: Manuel Azaña.

Republican Union: slightly to the right of Republican Left.

    Leader: Diego Martínez Barrios.

Catalan Left (Esquerra): social policies similar to Republican Left, but with emphasis on autonomy of Catalonia as independent Republic.

    Leader: Luis Companys.

Galician Federation: social policies similar to Republican Left, but with emphasis on autonomy of Galicia as independent Republic ; now part of Republican Left.

    Leader: Santiago Casares Quiroga.

Socialist Party: considers immediate task to be defeat of fascism, but has ultimate goal of collective form of government with socialisation of production.

    Leaders: Francisco Largo Caballero (Left), Indalecio Prieto (Centre), and Julian Besteiro (Right).

Communist Party: Considers immediate task to be fulfilment of democratic republic, but has ultimate goal of workers' and peasants' State with Soviet form of government.

    Leader: José Diaz.

Unified Socialist Party of Catalonia (Partit Socialista Unificat de Catalunya[1]—P.S.U.C.): merger of

[1] In Catalan.

Catalan Socialists and Communists; affiliated with Communist International.

> *Leaders:* Joan Comorera and M. Valdes.

Iberian Anarchist Federation (Federación Anarquista Ibérica—F.A.I.): for " libertarian communism "; opposed to all State power; official anti-People's-Front position weakening, especially among rank and file.

> *Leaders:* Buenaventura Durruti, Juan García Oliver and Angel Pestaña.

Workers' Party of Marxist Unification (Partido Obrero de Unificación Marxista—P.O.U.M.): main emphasis against Communist Party; led by expelled Communists; strong Trotskyist influence; anti-People's-Front.

> *Leaders:* Andrés Nin and Joaquin Maurin.

CENTRE

Radical Party: extreme Right petty-bourgeois; ally of fascist parties; strongly anti-Socialist.

> *Leader:* Alejandro Lerroux.

Conservative Party: slightly to the right of Radical Party; pro-clerical.

> *Leader:* Miguel Maura.

Liberal Democratic Party: minor reactionary group.

> *Leader:* Melquiades Alvarez.

RIGHT

Spanish Confederation of Autonomous Right Parties (Confederación Española de Derechas Autónomas—C.E.D.A.): Right coalition from reactionary republicans to monarchists under fascist leadership.

> *Leaders:* José Maria Gil Robles and José Calvo Sotelo (deceased).

Popular Action (Acción Popular): fascist; strongly pro-clerical.

Leader: José Maria Gil Robles.

Agrarian Party: defends interests of largest landowners; strongly pro-clerical.

Leader: José Martínez de Velasco.

Spanish Regeneration (Renovación Española): restoration of Alfonso XIII based on fascist regime.

Leaders: Antonio Goicoechea and José Calvo Sotelo.

Spanish Phalanx (Falange Española): openly fascist on Nazi model.

Leader: José Antonio Primo de Rivera.

Carlists (Traditionalists): followers, since 1833, of line of Don Carlos, brother of Fernando VII, who pretended to throne against Isabel II; opposed to Alfonso XIII; strongly clerical and reactionary.

Basque Nationalist Party: for measure of autonomy to Basque Provinces; strongly clerical and reactionary, with Carlist leanings.

Leader: José Horn.

Catalan Regionalist League (Liga Regionalista Catala): strongly conservative, but regionalist; in opposition to Catalan Left.

Leaders: Francisco Cambó and Juan Ventosa.

TRADE UNIONS

General Workers' Union (Unión General de Trabajadores —U.G.T.): led by Left Socialists and Communists.

National Confederation of Labour (Confederación Nacional de Trabajo): led by anarcho-syndicalists.